BIPOLAR, EPILEPTIC PAPA AND BUSINESSMAN

by

Bruce Bowman

DORRANCE
PUBLISHING CO
EST. 1920
PITTSBURGH, PENNSYLVANIA 15238

Dorrance Publishing Co
585 Alpha Drive
Suite 103
Pittsburgh, PA 15238
Visit our website at *www.dorrancebookstore.com*

ISBN: 979-8-8860-4152-1
eISBN: 979-8-8860-4808-7

TABLE OF CONTENTS

Why did I put my life story in print?

In my lifetime I have gone through many emotions starting from my childhood exhilaration and frustration to reward and self-doubt, to runner's highs, to grand mal epileptic seizures, to bipolar depression, consisting of both highs and lows, and now geriatric contentment. As I progress to the ripe age of seventy-four, I have witnessed parts of five generations of my family, and possibly six before I am gone forever. I was fortunate to share the lives of my grandparents, except Dad's mom, my parents, my siblings, my children, my grandchildren, and hopefully a great-grandchild or two. When I started writing, I soon realized that I knew very little about my grandparents and parents before my arrival. It is too late.... They are gone with all their memories and history. I am writing my life story so my family and future family can understand me a little better, and what things were like in my generation. You cannot write once you are no longer here, at least not yet. Also, because I have gone through mental illnesses, I chose to make my life the best I could, although it was challenging, I would like to share it.

I have recently been inspired by Jamie Raskin, a Maryland Congressman from the 8th district. A Harvard Law School graduate, he was the lead impeachment manager for the 2nd impeachment of Donald Trump. He and his son Tommy were very close to one another. Tommy took his own life at the age of twenty-five because of mental illness, including depression and obsessive-compulsive disorder.

This was totally heartbreaking for Jamie, his family, and his friends. Tommy was very bright and was in his second year at Harvard Law School when this unfortunate incident happened. After his son's suicide, Jamie questioned himself. "What could I have done to prevent this?" "What is depression? I don't understand it." Jamie had never battled depression. He battled Stage 3 colon cancer in 2010 exposing himself to grueling rounds of radiation and chemotherapy and afterward, he had an overwhelming desire to live. Tommy's depression was so different. Jamie had an MRI approximately three months after Tommy's death to determine if the growth on his stomach was cancerous. An MRI is an electronic device that details images of organs and tissues in your body. It is a long, narrow cylinder, that encloses your body during the imaging process. While having the MRI Jamie thought of Tommy and his depression.

Jamie, being claustrophobic, was very concerned about taking this MRI, which lasted thirty-seven minutes. His thoughts were of how Tommy felt when he was in depression. That thirty-seven minutes seemed an eternity to Jaimie. He compared these thirty-seven minutes to Tommy's depression although Jamie knew he could walk out of the doctor's office once the imaging was finished, Tommy felt his only escape from his unrelenting disease, was suicide. (Notes from a Washington Post article by Caitlin Gibson, 12/6/2021)

Being bipolar and suffering from suicidal tendencies, I planted an early thought in my head when I was feeling normal that I would never commit suicide because of my wonderful wife, Evelyn, and my loving kids, Jennifer, Jill, and Jeff. This thought was reinforced over and over again in my mind. When I had thoughts of suicide, they were erased. It wasn't easy. Depression has strong willpower. Now that I am finally on the right medication, I no longer have thoughts of suicide. I encourage anyone aware of a person who is thinking of suicide to reach out to that person and get them to promise they will not commit suicide. Be direct and bold. That promise may save a life.

In 1976, I was twenty-eight years old, two years into my marriage to Evelyn, father of our first daughter Jennifer, and living in Maui, Hawaii. In addition, we were at the very beginning of our new business, Maui Fumigation. It was this same year that I was diagnosed as having epilepsy. Twelve years later I started suffering from major depression and later diagnosed as bipolar 2.

My depression was severe due to anxiety and lack of sleep. At times, I couldn't go to work for months, and then there were times I felt perfectly normal. In one of my "perfectly normal" periods, I thought of opening a second office on the Island of Hawaii, in the beautiful city of Hilo. Our three kids were all grown up by this time, so Evelyn and I endeavored this task. We had good help and our second office was established although it was quite stressful. My depression returned unthankfully and frequently. I saw a psychiatrist in Hilo. Over the years, several psychiatrists said my condition was depression but nothing they were prescribing was solving my downward spirals.

Eventually, after help from my sister Pam, I told my psychiatrist that I may be bipolar. Finally, after some reluctance on his part, he agreed that I was suffering from bipolar 2 disorder. This condition is not resolved by antidepressants alone, although that was his only recommendation for an additional two years. I continued to suffer from bipolar depression, and it was getting worse.

Evelyn and I moved from Hilo back to Maui. I contacted another psychiatrist. He was aware I was bipolar but still recommended antidepressants and eventually shock therapy because I wasn't getting any better. After one year on Maui and no change in my mental state, I sought out another psychiatrist. In our first session, he asked if I had ever been on a mood stabilizer. My response was "No, the other psychiatrists never mentioned mood stabilizers." He put me on Lithium and Seroquel. That was the missing link.

I am a lucky guy now. Living with mental disorders and trying to support a wonderful family and a successful business was very challenging. I did it, and I am a very proud Bipolar, Epileptic, Papa, and Businessman, and would like to share my life with you.

CHAPTER 1

My Grandparents, Aunts, Uncles, Mom and Dad before I was Born 1914–1948

Some of my family information was obtained from Ancestry.com and a little from my sisters Julie and Pam, and my cousin, Jan. Some I obtained while growing up but much of it is blank, just not there.

Grandparents and Aunts and Uncles

My mother's parents: My grandfather was (Chester) Arthur Haight and my grandmother was Jessie Haight. They divorced when my mom was about eighteen. Grandfather remarried after moving to Kansas. His new wife, Meta, and he purchased an eighty-acre farm in Winchester Kansas and grew wheat. Mom, Dad, Bonnie, and I went to Kansas to visit Grandpa and Meta when I was a youngster. I remember my grandpa kept his britches up with suspenders and wore a crinkled hat like Jed Clampett of *The Beverly Hillbillies*. He was on the pudgy side. His stomach protruded and it looked like a punching bag, so I punched it. He didn't like that, so he punched me back. I was shocked; then I cried. My step-grandmother, Meta, was a terrible cook, not like Mom. For breakfast, we would have hominy grits and a small piece of dry meat, for lunch, we would have a sandwich made of the same dry meat, and for dinner, we would get a bigger piece of the same dry meat and black-eyed peas and your choice of potatoes, boiled or mashed. I didn't have a choice except for the potatoes. Mom made us clean our plates. I was afraid to ask what the dried meat was. That trip was the only time I saw Grandpa and Meta. I never saw them again.

Mom's mom, Grandma Jessie, planned to live with us at our Rosemead house in a cottage that my dad had built, but she changed her mind. I think she was going through depression. I was probably eight or nine at the time. To the best of my recollection, I never saw her again after her trip to California. Grandma was not a warm person, and I don't even recall her laughing. I was young and probably did not pay enough attention.

Grandma Jessie's maiden name was Kemp, Mom's oldest brother was Uncle Kemp, named after his mother, and my middle name is Kemp. Next to Uncle Kemp was Aunt Dorothy and then Mom, born December 19, 1916, and finally Uncle Bob. They lived in Sparks, Nevada. Uncle Kemp was my favorite. One Christmas he and Aunt Helen came to visit. He put $5 in each one of our stockings. That was a lot of money in those days. As soon as I could, I put it in the bank. Uncle Kemp had a lot of personality and everyone was his friend. Mom said he was a very good football player in high school. Uncle Bob, the youngest, was in the military and came to see us a few times. He was very likable and easygoing. I vaguely recall Aunt Dorothy; I know she and Mom didn't see eye to eye. We rarely saw my aunts and uncles and cousins. It is not like Hawaii where our extended family is together all the time. They lived in Nevada, and we lived in California.

My grandfather on my father's side was Bruce L. Bowman, born in 1892 in Lexington, Kentucky and my grandmother was Emma Hays Bowman, born in 1894. They were married in 1913 and my dad was born on October 25, 1914. My grandfather was in the excavating business and did well. The business was made up of his brothers and was called the Bowman Brothers. The Bowman Brothers even did work in India. My grandfather brought his young wife, Emma, his daughter Helen, and my dad with him. However, when in India, my grandmother was diagnosed with tuberculosis. According to my first cousin, Jan Siefert, daughter of my dad's sister Helen, she probably had tuberculosis before arriving in India. In 1920 she was put on an ocean liner back to California with her two children, my dad and Aunt Helen. She was hoping for rest and recuperation.

My grandfather was notified she was dying. He came home via the Indian Ocean and the Suez Canal. She never recuperated and died in 1921, before Granddad's arrival. She was just twenty-six years old. Dad was just six years old. He and Aunt Helen were raised by Emma's mother. Granddad remarried in 1926 to his bride, Dorothy, whom I admired. Together they had three children, my aunt Dorothy, uncle Dick, and aunt Mary. Dad, for some reason, wanted his kids to call his stepmom Aunt Dot. Dad was already twelve at the time of their marriage. His younger brothers and sisters were considerably younger. I don't recall stories of his childhood. It must have been a very tough life for my grandparents. They grew up during the Great Depression 1929–1933 and I am in the dark about their lives during this time. My dad was fifteen when the stock market crashed. Grandfather was still in the excavation business, but I think he lost everything. I wish I knew. In the early '50s, as I was growing up, I remember my grandfather being tall, over six feet. My dad and I must have gotten our height genes from Emma, Dad's mother. We were both around 5'7".

Grandad and Aunt Dot lived about twenty miles from our Rosemead house in North Hollywood. Their house was old and somewhat unkempt. By the time I was nine or ten, my grandfather was suffering from severe arthritis in his right hand and almost always wore old pajamas and sat in his chair. He generally had at least three days of whiskers on his face. He would rarely move. I know he was suffering from depression, although I had no concept of depression at that time. Aunt Dot was subservient to him and his grouchy needs. I was Aunt Dot's pet, and I loved her attention. She was a great storyteller; however, I wish she had written a biography of her life and my grandfather. She was a great writer. Now it is too late. She outlived him for many years. When I was ten years old, she started me with a coin collection and gave me a coin album and some of her collection. Unfortunately, I didn't get involved in the coin collecting. I will pass it on to one of my grandchildren. I was more into baseball cards. Aunt Dot was bright, joyful, and very interesting.

Mom

Mom was born on December 19, 1916, in Ogden, Utah. I know very little of her life other than what I experienced. Both my father's and mother's childhood were rarely discussed. Being the last child, you don't always get all the family stories. I do know that she was a high school graduate from Sparks, Nevada. After high school, she went to beauty school and became a beautician. From Nevada, she moved west. She came to California with her mother who just recently divorced my grandfather and got a job as she wished in Hollywood. Hollywood may sound glitzy, but most of Hollywood is not glitzy. Where Mom and Dad and my grandparents were, was not glitzy. Mom was attractive with beautiful blue eyes and a nice figure.

One year after they got married their lives changed with the start of World War II. World War II began on September 1, 1939, in Europe when Nazi Germany, under Adolf Hitler invaded Poland. From 1939 to 1941 Germany conquered or controlled much of continental Europe. The involvement by the United States was minimal at this time. Japan, Italy, and Nazi Germany formed the major nations of the Axis, opposing the Allies, the most important nations of Allies were led by Great Britain, France, except during the German occupation, the Soviet Union, China, and the United States.

Japan got very aggressive as it wanted to dominate Asia and the Pacific. Japan bombed Pearl Harbor on December 7, 1941. The United States declared war on Japan. The European Axis powers declared war on the United States. Japan captured much of the western Pacific, but its advances were halted after losing a critical battle in Midway in 1942. Germany and Italy were defeated in North Africa and Stalingrad in the Soviet Union. By 1943 Germany and Italy were on the retreat. In 1944 the Western Allies invaded German-occupied France, while the Soviet Union turned towards Germany and its allies. Japan was suffering setbacks in mainland Asia while the Allies crippled the Japanese Navy. The war in Europe concluded with the liberation of the German-occupied territories and the invasion of Germany by the Western Allies and the Soviet Union. This culminated in the fall of Berlin to the Soviet troops, the suicide of Hitler, and the German surrender on May 8, 1945. Japan refused to surrender on US terms. On August 6, 1945, and August 9, 1945, Hiroshima and Nagasaki were bombed with the first atomic bombs. With the atomic bombings and more bombings possibly to come, and the threat of the Soviet Union entering the war against Japan, Japan's surrender document was signed on September 2, 1945. (Help from Wikipedia)

My sister, Julie revealed a story to me. She was 3½ years old, and she and Mom stood out in their small backyard in North Hollywood watching the military planes fly overhead. Mom was crying and when Julie asked her "Why are you crying, Mom?" She responded, "My brother will be able to come home from the war." That was my uncle Bob who made the military his career. Rather ironic, Uncle Bob eventually took a Japanese wife.

Dad

Dad was two years older than Mom. He was born in Missouri on October 25, 1914. Dad and Mom lived through some very tough times. Just before Dad's arrival, World War I was just taking hold in Europe, and it lasted for the first four years of his life. In 1918 the Spanish Flu, a major pandemic spread throughout the world causing major casualties. I have very little information about his childhood. I know it was tough, without his mother Emma, and living with his sister, the two had to often fare for themselves. The stock market crashed a few days after his fifteenth birthday while in his sophomore year. That was in October of 1929. Some people lost their fortunes, some people lost their jobs, and some people lost their lives.

Dad was fortunate. He finished the 11th grade at Hollywood High. That was good considering all the difficulties. President Roosevelt commissioned the CCC (Civil Conservation Corp). It was part of the New Deal to help lift the United States out of the Great Depression. It was for unemployed single men of the ages of eighteen years to enlist in work programs to improve America's public lands, forests, and parks. When Dad turned eighteen, he joined the CCC. This program provided the workers with shelter, clothing, and food and $30 per month, $25 of which had to be sent home to their families. History looks favorably upon the CCC. Dad must have enjoyed it because he loved the outdoors and doing handy work. The morale was high among those recruited. When Dad finished his time in the CCC, he eventually met Mom. My parents met and were married not too long afterward in 1938. Mom was twenty-one and Dad was twenty-four.

They rented a small house in North Hollywood. Dad, at the time, was working in a dry-cleaning business, and Mom was a beautician. They wanted to raise a family but put that on hold initially because money was tight. Julie, my firstborn sister, was a war baby born on April 9, 1942, she was later joined by Pat and Pam, her twin fraternal sisters. They were also war babies, born on March 3, 1945, six months before the end of the war. Raising three girls in a small home in North Hollywood was getting a little crowded. They looked for land to build a bigger house. They found just what they were looking for in Rosemead, an unincorporated city, approximately twelve miles east of Los Angeles, in the San Gabriel Valley. They purchased a commercial ½ acre of land just east of Rosemead Blvd. on Glendon Way. A commercial ½ acre is about 18,000 square feet. It was a nice-sized lot in which Dad could build a nice house, large enough for his growing family. He had plenty of room for a vegetable garden and playing horseshoes and a lot more. There was a small existing house that Dad remodeled and enlarged. Little did they know that my twin Bonnie and I were coming.

CHAPTER 2

Mom and Dad in My Lifetime? 1948–1991

Dad was Bernard Bruce Bowman and his friends called him Bernie and Mom was born Bessie Haight; her friends called her Kit. She hated her given name Bessie because when she was small, bullies called her Bessie the cow. She was a little overweight when she was younger. So, Kit and Bernie are my parents. Mom lost that chubbiness and never regained it. She was always trim and fit.

When I was born on June 27, 1948, I had four sisters. My oldest sister Julie was six years older than me, Pat and Pam, fraternal twins, were three years older than me, and Bonnie, my twin, was four minutes older than me. I don't remember that day well, but I certainly realized that I needed to become independent. I wasn't going to be a sissy. I kept wondering, where is my brother? Maybe Mom and Dad will make one for me. Not a chance in HELL. They didn't expect Bonnie and me. So, five kids, two sets of twins, Bonnie and I, infants, Pat and Pam, three-year-old, and Julie, a six-year-old, were more than they bargained for. My dad had a terrible time with our names, in fact with anyone's names. He called us all honey. Yes, I was called honey. I have a similar problem; I get my grandkids mixed up. He passed this gene on to me as I have done to my son Jeff.

While we were growing up, Dad was our family's sole provider. In those days wives often stayed home to raise the kids. Dad made a modest income for a family of seven, five kids plus him and Mom. He worked hard and he was very good at what he did. The first job I remember, he was the Chief Inspector for Southwest Engineering Company near or in Los Angeles, about twenty miles from our home. This was in the 1950s and 1960s. As the company's Chief Inspector, his work was quality control. His company made large tanks, vessels, boilers, and other containers that hold liquids and gasses. He would inspect his company's merchandise by analyzing the welds and rivets and whatever other methods were used in their assembly. Dad was on a monthly salary and as I recall it was $750 per month, which was probably much less than the unionized boilermakers whose work he was inspecting. Dad had two weeks of paid vacation, which I think eventually became three. Those vacations were always spent with our family on camping and fishing expeditions. What I remember most about Southwest Engineering were the annual company parties. I remember having so much fun and we could drink soda and we didn't have to stop at one. We could eat three ice cream cones if we so desired. There was popcorn and hot dogs and candy and other good junk food and games. I am sure Mom enjoyed it because we were out of sight. Dad worked with Southwest Engineering for quite some time. I am guessing that he was there for twenty-five to thirty years. In his last few years of work, he worked for Bechtel Engineering before his retirement.

Mom was a typical housewife in the 1950s and 1960s. She did not work in a paid job, but she worked very hard raising us five kids. She managed the income that my father generated, and she was squeaky tight, and I mean squeaky. Justifiably so. Mom sewed a lot of the girls' clothes and cooked nearly all our meals. She was a good cook except for the cauliflower that I hated. She made us clean our plates and I would gag when the overcooked, mushy cauliflower was on the menu. She packed our sack lunches until we reached a certain age and then we packed our own. We would get a nickel per day for our milk. We all had chores and we had to make our beds in the morning. Our presents on our birthday or Christmas were very modest. We didn't feel cheated. Only me. On my eighth birthday, I wanted a baseball glove so bad. I got it, but the stuffing was falling out and it only had three fingers and a thumb like a Mickey Mouse hand. I cried.

Dad was rather easygoing unless he got mad, but it was not often he got mad at us kids. Mom was the disciplinarian. However, the two of them could get into heated arguments. Mom and Dad would raise their voices with each other and then yelling would start. At that point, Dad would storm out of the house to his workshop and vent. They would both cool off and reunite as if nothing happened. Their arguments were generally over finances or that Mom was getting bossy with him. It didn't take much for my mom to lose her temper. She had a very short fuse.

If she wasn't in the right mood, she could be rattled very easily. I could rattle her by being in the same room. We bumped heads a lot. She had her caring moments too and her good significantly outweighed her bad.

I think I took more after my mom. She was good with the girls, especially Bonnie but parenting wasn't easy for her. Both Mom and Dad had strong values. Honesty, reliability, respectfulness, timeliness, and many other good values were all highly emphasized in raising us. Mom would take us to the Unity Church, and we would go to Sunday School. I rather enjoyed it. Unity is a very liberal church compared to most. The Unity Church teaches Heaven and Hell are not places you go to after death but experience them in your consciousness here on earth. Satan is not a physical entity. Satan exists in your conscience. Also, the Unity Church is very accepting of all people including gays, lesbians, and transgender. In addition to our values, we were brought up with good work ethics. We didn't shy away from hard work. We were raised with good principles.

It wasn't all work; we had a lot of fun together as a family. We celebrated the traditional birthdays and holidays together and we went to Rosemead High football games, Girl Scout outings, and summer trips together. Yes, I went to Girl Scout outings because my four sisters were Girl Scouts. We were a close family and on rare occasions, we would jump into the car and get Morgan's homemade ice cream. Freezers were very small in those days. I didn't know anybody who had two refrigerators. At least we were better off than our parents in their younger days they had to continually buy ice for their iceboxes.

CHAPTER 3

Hanabata Days 1955–1963

When I was in my hanabata days. What days? Hanabata days.

In Hawaiian Pidgin English, hana in Japanese means nose, and bata is butter, so nose butter days. In simple terms, runny nose days. I wasn't in Hawaii, but beautiful Rosemead. I was a rascal, a brat, and the youngest and only boy with four sisters. It was a real challenge growing up. To make it worse, I was a real crybaby too. If I were the father of this hanabata boy, I would have been upset with this rascal kid often, just like my mom was. Dad was at work while Mom took care of us during the summers.

Rosemead was a middle-class neighborhood. Our house was about one mile south of Rosemead High School and twelve miles east of Los Angeles. We were approximately thirty miles from the Pacific Ocean and if you went east you may arrive in Palm Springs if you took the right turns. If you went north, you would be in the San Gabriel Mountains. We were very centrally located. I have some good and not-so-good memories of this time. One time my sisters were playing jacks outside on our concrete walkway and a honeybee came near them. They were screaming and making all sorts of commotion. I came to their rescue and stepped on the bee, then I screamed and cried, and cried some more. I was barefoot.

When I was even younger, I came to their rescue on another occasion. I was probably four years old at the time and I saved them from two fighting dogs. I tried to break up the dog fight because I was macho; I got bit in the face and my dad and mom had to take me to the emergency room to get stitched up. The last place my mom wanted to take any of us was to the hospital because it was expensive. She was very upset with me. I thought she would be grateful to me for protecting my sisters. She wasn't grateful; she thought I was stupid.

Another memorable experience I had when I was either ten or eleven is when I climbed a chain-link fence to get an overthrown football. The fence was about six feet high and I was probably four feet tall. As I reached the top my arm got caught on one of the V-shaped prongs. My arm was cut nearly to the bone. I had a six-inch gash bleeding profusely. I didn't know what to do because I couldn't tell my mom she would be furious. I didn't tell her. I wore long sleeve shirts even though it was summer. After a while, I realized my gash wasn't healing properly because of the infection. I was going to have to face the consequences. I never saw a doctor and she did her best to make it better. She used some Merthiolate and some Mercurochrome, and within weeks the infection declined. The scar remains until today, however the first few years it was very pronounced and purplish. This time my mom was a little more sympathetic, I guess I caught her in the right mood. Mom was much better with the girls. Boys are generally much more daring and adventuresome. I was not a wimp; it wasn't in my genes.

Another memorable experience occurred over the next winter. Winters in Rosemead can be quite chilly in the morning. It could be freezing. Our house was not heated except for our fireplace and a furnace at the end of the hallway. In the cold mornings, all five of us kids would dart to the furnace and fight for the best positioning. Our winter days could be sunny in the afternoons. After school, I'd always play sports with my friends. You can't play sports with a jacket on so I would take it off. On four occasions that winter, I took my jacket off to play sports and I couldn't find where I put it, or I forgot it completely. Losing jackets was not cheap and my mom was on a tight budget. She was not a happy camper with me. If I were younger, she would have probably spanked me with a pancake-turner, as she used to, or maybe I would be sent to my room. When I was sent to my room, I would sneak a potato out of the kitchen and play with Mr. Potato Head. Now she just had to scold me, and I would cry. I was very sensitive. I would have rather gone to my room. In the'50s, spanking was even common in schools. If you had to go to the principal's office, be prepared.

One of our more memorable experiences growing up during the summer was my fishing outings to Legg Lake. Legg Lake is about four miles from our Rosemead house. Dennis Smith and I would ride our bikes, take our fishing poles and our tackle boxes, and fish at the water inlet. The lake would be stocked periodically with trout. They were usually between six and eight inches. Once in a great while you might get lucky and get a fat one of ten inches. If you had a bad day and didn't catch any trout, you could go to the other side of the lake and catch some boney crappies. They were about three to four inches long and not worth cleaning. One time I was in our garage and noticed this strange smell and in addition, I also noticed these little white things crawling on the garage floor. I soon realized that the white crawling things were maggots, and they were coming from my tackle box from the dead trout that I forgot to clean a week ago. Now the flies were cleaning them just as nature intended. Why did nature put out such a terrible stench? This tackle box was handed down from my sister Julie. It was her jewelry box and now it is my smelly tackle box. I eventually quit hanging around with Dennis Smith. He was Catholic and he said that because I wasn't Catholic, I was going to go to Hell.

I was with my dad when I caught my first fish. Dad loved fishing. I think we were at Twin Lakes, near Mammoth, California. He took me hiking along a little stream. We came across a small pond about ten feet in diameter. There was a lot of vegetation with low branches all around. We silently approached the pond. Dad threw in the line with a bobber and a hook with salmon eggs, and he handed the pole to me. The bobber went down instantaneously, I jerked the pole, and out came my catch. In my excitement, this little six-inch brook trout went on a real journey wrapping around a branch about four times. We were able to untangle it with considerable effort. I think it was the same day when we returned to our campsite, Dad was chopping wood to build a campfire. I pleaded with him to let me chop wood. He was hesitant but gave in to my persistence. On the very first swing of the ax, I almost cut my left index finger off. I didn't hit the wood right and the ax ricocheted smack into my finger. I still have the scar to prove it.

Another fishing experience with my dad was when we visited my grandfather, Chester, and my step-grandmother, Meta on my mother's side. It was a hot muggy day in Winchester, Kansas and we were trying to catch catfish. I was bored; I don't remember if we did, that wasn't the memorable part. I remember laying down by the lakeside and getting chiggers all over my body. You don't feel them at first. Chiggers are very small mites that are hardly visible to the human eye. Their diet is animal tissue and that day it was mine. They don't suck blood. They generally need something to compress themselves to the body. They commonly bite under the beltline, on ankles compressed by your socks, and on wrinkles in your skin. I think I had them everywhere. They cause such an intense itch and I scratched until I bled. It certainly was not a nice experience driving back to California in the middle of the summer with no air conditioning with chigger bites all over your body. I was miserable.

Other hanabata memories include going to Boulevard Cleaners and getting free bubble gum. There were two ladies that I particularly remember. One lady was mean and certainly didn't like hanabata kids and the other was very nice. If you went into Boulevard Cleaners and the mean lady was at the counter, you would do an about-face and walk out. If the nice lady was at the counter, you were in luck. I think my chances were about 50/50. The bubble gum was pink, and the sweet flavor lasted about five minutes. After a short time of chewing, you could blow bubbles. If you were lucky enough to get two pieces you could blow great big bubbles, the kind that when they popped, would stick to your face. It was easy to peel the gum off your face but when you got in your hair that was more difficult.

During my hanabata days, I rarely spent time with my sisters. If the sun was up, I was out playing. I had friends such as Dennis Mozoleski and Dennis Smith and Steve Presley, but I could entertain myself in the backyard by being with nature. I do remember playing jacks with my sisters or Monopoly, Sorry, or Clue. I didn't like to lose at anything and if I lost, I was a poor loser. Being the youngest I lost a lot and being a poor loser, they didn't want to play with me. I was fine with that; I didn't want to play with them either. I would go out and play with my slingshot. I had a Wham-O slingshot that I purchased with my allowance and over the summer I became quite proficient with it. Initially, I shot cans and bottles. I tried everything for ammo. Rocks weren't very good; they wouldn't go straight, and the right size was hard to find. Walnuts were too big, and small unripe apricots were pretty good, but nothing compared to marbles. Marbles were perfect and I could go to the "five and ten cents" store and buy a bunch for a dime. My choice of ammo became marbles. Our yard in Rosemead was quite large. Our neighbors on the left were the grouchy Bixlers, behind us were the Kaisers and on the right was Alice. The Bixlers were a strange old couple. Their yard was fenced in with a cheap wire fence with big openings. They had two barking boxers. Boxers are generally a friendly breed however these two were not. It could have been because once I threw a dirt clod and hit one of them in the face. Growing up I only saw Mr. Bixler occasionally. Mr. Bixler would be out in their unkempt yard at times, but he would not acknowledge my existence, never a pleasantry. In addition to the barking boxers, they had a pigeon coop towards their backyard, parallel with our walnut trees. There were probably twenty pigeons that would fly freely in and out of their coop. What a temptation. I took that temptation one time. I pulled my slingshot out and aimed at a pigeon with a trusty marble in the pouch and released it. I missed the pigeon but hit the coop. I didn't realize Mr. Bixler was outside. He heard the bang when the marble hit the coop. His awkward body was running towards me with his hands in the air shaking and him yelling, "Never do that again, you rascal!" I never did it again and I never threw dirt clods at the boxers again. I found something more fun to do. I would shoot my slingshot at sparrows and some stray cats. I was getting very good with my Wham-O. We had plenty of sparrows in those days because they would frequent the pigeon coop since there was always available food, but I would never shoot in that direction again. They would land in our walnut trees, apricot, or grapefruit trees. When the apricots got ripe, the sparrows were very abundant. When I aimed near the Kaiser house, I had to make sure that my trajectory would be low enough not to hit it. Once I didn't and I heard glass break. I don't know what I hit because I ran as fast as I could. Alice's house was in the safe zone. The worst thing when shooting my Wham-O is when the rubber breaks. You would get smacked in the face and that hurts. I learned what they meant when I was a freshman, "Never let your rubbers break."

There were times that I would be with my sisters during the summer. Bonnie, Pat, Pam, and I would walk to Savannah Elementary School and get involved in some form of supervised play. I don't remember Julie going, in fact, I vaguely remember Julie during our childhood. I don't think she wanted to associate with us. She was a teenager. We all learned to play ping-pong. Pam and I played the most and we got pretty good at it. When I was tired of ping-pong, I would go outside and play basketball, spin my top, or play with my yo-yo. When none of my friends were watching, I would play with the hula hoop, play hopscotch, or jump rope; I liked it when we had the double ropes. We always had something to do. Sometimes I would play with my Slinky, or get out my Silly Putty and throw it against the wall to see if it would stick. With the boys, not a game for girls, I would play marbles. If

I had a bad day in marbles, maybe I'd go fly a kite as my mom always told me to do. "Go fly your kite." She would say that when I was getting on her nerves. We always had something to do in those days. Our toys were very inexpensive, and we had fun. There was very little obesity. Kids were busy; we had (PE) physical education every school day. We would play tetherball, volleyball, basketball, football, kickball you name it; if it had a ball, we would play it. Mom and Dad also got involved in our activities. Dad made a shuffleboard court at our Rosemead house.

We had a basketball hoop, we played ping-pong, croquet, and various other games together at our house. Mom was a pretty good athlete, well… not really, but she was knowledgeable of how sports were played, more so than Dad, but she couldn't play horseshoes as he did. He was just a so-so athlete, but he was just tremendous at horseshoes. He would come home after work and practice on our horseshoe pit. He got to the point where he could average a ringer, one out of three tosses. In those days we didn't have cell phones or computers or nearly as many automobiles, but we were always actively playing and trying to get better at different events. I rode my bicycle everywhere I wanted to go, but once I entered high school nobody rode bikes, because it wasn't cool.

I started playing organized baseball when I was eight years old. My friend Steve's dad, Mr. Cooley, was our minor league coach. He was a Marine who fought in WWII against the Japanese on the battlefield. He wasn't the typical Marine. He was soft-spoken and patient with us youngsters and a great coach. Our sponsor was Earl and Emil Texaco on Rosemead Blvd. If we won a game, we would get to go to the Dairy Queen and get treated to a nickel ice cream cone. That was a real treat. I was just okay at baseball. I played for four years and realized it was no hope for me. I wasn't going to make the pros. I was a much better fan. At ten years old, I fell in love with the Los Angeles Dodgers. The Dodgers moved from Brooklyn to LA in 1958. LA only had minor league baseball teams before that. I listened to every Dodger game I could on my transistor radio and I would fall asleep listening, fighting sleep the whole way. Vince Scully and Jerry Doggett were the announcers. Vince Scully mesmerized me. He was so good and brought the game in full vision over the radio. The games usually started at 8:00 p.m. and there was pregame coverage and postgame coverage. I listened to every minute of the games until I would fall asleep; sometimes I managed to make it through to completion.

One such game was August 31, 1959, and Sandy Kofax was the pitcher for the Dodgers and was facing San Francisco, their archrival. Kofax had a whizzing fastball and a wicked curve. The game was a thriller. There were 82,794 fans in the LA Coliseum. In the top of the eighth inning, the Dodgers were behind 2–1 and Kofax had fifteen strikeouts. In the bottom of the eighth inning, the Dodgers tied the score. In the top of the ninth, Kofax struck out the 16th batter. I would run into the living room to tell Mom "He struck out sixteen!" A few minutes later I ran to the living room again, "He struck out seventeen!" Seventeen strikeouts in a nine-inning game tied the National League record. The next batter he faced, Kofax recorded his 18th strikeout, striking out the side. Guess what? I ran to my mom, "He struck out eighteen!" Kofax broke the National League record. I was elated, but the game wasn't over. It was still 2–2. The Dodgers came up in the bottom of the ninth, with one out and runners on first and third, Wally Moon came to the plate and hit a three-run homer—Dodgers 5 San Francisco 2—what a tremendous game.

I was hooked on baseball and Mom became a big fan. We had something in common. Dad wasn't really into sports as much as Mom, other than horseshoes. Over the years we went to several Dodger games and Mom and Dad attended almost all the Rosemead High School football games while we were kids because Pat and Pam and, eventually Bonnie were varsity cheerleaders. Mom and Dad and especially me took a real interest in football. On November 22, 1963, President John F. Kennedy was assassinated. Rosemead High had a game that night. Fortunately, it wasn't canceled. We went to the game with tears and sobs throughout the game, but it was a real relief to get away from the news on our small black and white TV.

I played flag football, but Steve Cooley could play tackle football. Flag football was fun, but I couldn't wiggle my hips very well, so I was relegated to a non-ball carrying position. I also played football with my neighbors down the street, Steve Presley and Dennis Mozeleski.

CHAPTER 4

Jobs When I Was Young 1959–1963

Before having a real boss, I had several jobs in which I was my boss, or I should say, my mom was my boss. Growing up I had a lot of chores around the house and yard, but those don't count as jobs. I mowed our neighbor's lawn. Alice was a divorced middle-aged woman whose marriage didn't last due to her alcoholic, abusive husband. This was in Rosemead around 1959 and I was eleven. I started a paper route about a year later. The paper, *El Monte Valley Herald* came out two days a week, Saturdays and Thursdays. It had a little bit of local news but mostly ads. Thursday was the big ad day, and the papers could get heavy. The papers would be delivered to our house early in the morning and I would fold them and put them in two connected bags that fit over the handlebars of my bike. Then I would deliver the papers to my designated route. I had 140 papers and my customers were all within a five-block area. It was generally fast, I delivered to every house in my area unless they requested no paper. Do kids do paper routes anymore?

I remember one Thursday morning when I woke up late and the papers were especially thick that day. Mom was already getting mad at me because it appeared that I was going to be late for school. I was very frustrated. I had to fold them and put them into my paper bags. I could hardly get all the papers in the two bags. When I finally did, I tried picking up my bike with the paper bags full. As the tires slipped out, I was outraged. I was crying and not knowing what to do. This was my first major job crisis but I eventually got them delivered. I removed about 1/3 of the papers from the bags, delivered what I could that morning, and delivered the other 1/3 when I got home from school. I had never been late to school, so my teacher was understanding. My mom had cooled down and nobody complained about the late delivery. This crisis is over. Now I must learn from this experience.. Tom Delmore, my closest friend for the past forty-plus years, told me about his newspaper days. He grew up in Wisconsin. He delivered papers in the dead of winter through ice and snow and minus 20-degree temperature. If he fell into a ditch, he could have died from hypothermia. I look like a wimp compared to what he had to go through. So much for my thoughts that I was not a wimp.

The *El Monte Valley Herald* was free. However, we paperboys were requested to collect from our customers if we could. It was called "voluntary collection." We would go from door to door asking for a 35-cent donation. Our collections were turned over to our distributor. I was always very honest. I can't remember what I got paid, but it was more than my 50 cents allowance per week that I was getting. I was able to save my money and buy a three-speed bicycle. The first month I did well according to the paper standards collecting about 25% of my route. I collected nearly $12 and a few of the customers would even give me a small tip. I went to almost every house. Sometimes nobody was home, sometimes they would say they were not interested, and some didn't know what I was talking about. I remember this old man coming to the door and I quickly said, "Collecting for the *El Monte Valley Herald*." He asked, "What about olive oil?" At my current age, I can now relate.

As the months went by, collecting got harder. I hated collecting. Mom would ask, "Have you done your collections?" Each month my collections declined as I started only going to the houses where I wasn't rejected, and I could get a tip. I learned from this job. Jobs aren't always as easy as they appear.

Frank Suddarth was my first boss. My first job was in the summer before my freshman year at Rosemead High School. That would make it 1962. I was thirteen going on fourteen and I worked as a landscape gardener. We serviced the homes of the upper-middle class in the San Gabriel Valley. We provided lawn care and plant maintenance, generally every week, to many homes. Vic and Brice, Frank's parents, were very close friends with Mom and Dad. Often on the weekend they would get together and play Bridge. Brice would drive my mom crazy as many did. She had a rather high-pitched voice and a shrill laugh, and she would laugh a lot. Vic, on the other hand, was very quiet, serious, and patient. He had to be patient to live with Brice. I liked them both, and they seemed to be a very good match because their personalities were so opposite. They were our neighbors and lived on our street, Glendon Way, in Rosemead. Brice had one child from a former relationship and his name was Frank.

After Vic and Brice got married, they had a daughter, Connie. Connie was possibly eight years old when a tragedy happened. She stepped on a rusty nail and got tetanus and died. Connie and Julie, my sister, were best of friends. Connie's death was a real tragedy for all, especially for Vic, Brice, and Frank. I am sure their family went through some tough times. In addition to their loss of Connie, Frank eventually got into the wrong group at Rosemead High School and got into trouble. I don't know what he did, but it landed him in a juvenile correctional reform center. After he got out, he did reform. He grew up and became very responsible. When he was around twenty-three years old, he started a gardening service. It wasn't an easy start. The gardening business in Southern California was dominated by Japanese gardeners. They were good and their services were inexpensive. Frank persevered and his business grew.

Frank had a fun personality, and he was a hard worker. His gardening customers were spread out, so it allowed us time to talk while riding in his smelly yellow Ford 1959 Econovan, containing the gas-filled mowers and lawn edgers and all the necessary equipment to make a yard beautiful. There was no partition between the cargo and the cab. We got all the aromas such as steer manure, gasoline, fertilizer, pesticides, and whatever else. I enjoyed it, the smells, the work, Frank, and everything about it. I was proud. It was my first real job. I made $1.25 per hour. I was working outdoors with a fun boss. I was in heaven. I didn't have to be around my four sisters teasing and bothering me. On an average day, I would earn $10 and spend $1.00 for lunch. I netted 9 bucks a day, cash. (don't tell the IRS). That was a lot better than my 50 cents allowance per week when doing all my chores. I was very frugal with my money as my parents were and I was able to save most of it and made regular deposits to my bank account. Most of all, I enjoyed the work and I enjoyed Frank. One of the reasons Frank changed his rascal ways is because he met Pam, his beautiful wife. Pam had inner and outer beauty. She was always so nice to me.

At the time I started working with Frank, they had a baby daughter, a German Shepherd, and a small home. Frank taught me a lot about life. He would counsel me and give me good advice about growing up. "Don't get into gangs, play sports, study," he would say. He showed appreciation for my hard work, dependability, and honesty. He also taught me the love for gardening, which was not a preferred hobby for most teenagers in those days. I continue this appreciation for gardening and landscaping, as I have landscaped the homes that I have purchased and have always looked forward to doing yard maintenance. I listened to Frank, and I was a dependable worker, never missing a day. I worked hard and efficiently. Working for Frank only lasted one summer. In 1963 he sold his business and went to work for the railroad. I truly missed Frank.

Merle Beves was my second boss. In 1963 he purchased Frank's lawn care business and along with it came me during the summer and on Saturdays. Merle was not like Frank in any way. He was about 5'6" and always bent over due to a bum knee. He was slow and no fun. He was a rather grouchy sixty-plus or older man and didn't show any appreciation for what I did. It certainly wasn't the fun summer job that I had the previous year. I still enjoyed the work, however, the company I was keeping wasn't enjoyable. I realized that there is a big difference in a job when you work with someone who makes work fun and shows appreciation. I have tried to incorporate this mindset as an employer.

Merle would smoke his big cigars. He often lit up in the cab of the Econoline van. Now, I would inhale the cigar smoke, gasoline, pesticides, steer manure, and whatever else was in the van. I think I was somewhat used to it since both of my parents smoked. People weren't concerned about secondhand smoke in those days because so many people smoked, including a lot of teenagers. I was tempted and did sneak some cigarettes from my parents, but I did not like the image of me smoking and I didn't like the smell on my hands, so I resisted. I played sports and smoking was taboo.

When we got to our first stop, I would get out of the Econoline van, take a deep breath, and cough. My cough wasn't a result of aromas in the van, or the second-hand smoke, it was the air pollution outside, better known as SMOG. In the 1960s and 1970s, SMOG was at its worst in the Los Angeles area. It was always at its worst in the summer months. SMOG in the San Gabriel Valley was especially bad. The SMOG pollution was caused by industrial chemicals, but primarily from vehicle exhaust emissions. People in LA drove everywhere and all the time. The San Gabriel Mountains would trap the SMOG in the valley. The SMOG would cause your eyes to burn and when you inhaled, you would cough. Visibility would be reduced significantly. On a clear day in January, you may be able to see the San Gabriel Mountens ten miles away. On a smoggy day in August, you might be lucky to see thirty yards. Generally, the summer days are hot and dry with very little or no breeze. The temperature would go over 100F on many summer days. I remember seeing the thermometer go over 106F, now it goes higher due to global warming. Working outside in these conditions was tough. The smog combined with the heat would drain you, but I never missed a day of work.

Merle had two personalities. He was an avid bettor on horses, although he must have been a $2 bettor. During the week he would be in grubby clothes and dirty and dusty from the yard work. On Sundays, he dressed in his Sunday best and went to the Santa Anita racetrack to bet on the horses. That was his true love. He would trade in his dirty yellow dirty Econoline Van for his black shiny clean, "Stinkin Lincoln." It was nice. Merle looked dapper with his half-chewed cigar, clean clothes, and his shiny Lincoln. I don't know what he was trying to prove, he never appeared to have money, he rented an apartment with his wife, and he never once treated me to lunch. I missed Frank; he was so much more fun to work with. I think I worked for Merle for two summers and Saturdays. This job kept me in fairly good shape because when I went back to school, we would start football practice. The first two weeks were called "Hell Weeks" because they were. I was able to go through "Hell Weeks" better than most of my teammates because I had been working in the sun and breathing the SMOG all summer.

CHAPTER 5

My Sweat Days 1961–1966

My sweat days started about the time I entered Rosemead High School. It wasn't like the old days playing with my slingshot without a care in the world, I was now in high school, and my body was going through changes, and I didn't have the confidence that I had as a youngster. I did become freshman class president because Pat and Pam encouraged me to get involved in school. Pat and Pam were juniors and Bonnie and I were freshmen. In addition to her cheerleading, Pam was our Student Body President among 1000 other things and Pat was our homecoming princess among 750 other things. I wasn't quite ready as a student as a freshman. My body was changing, but slower than my peers. I looked like I was in 7th grade and some of my classmates looked like they were ready to graduate. I was short, about 5'3", and weighed 110 pounds dripping wet. Talk about wet, my underarms were always soaking wet, and I had big sweat rings on my shirts. I didn't have to be hot either. This was embarrassing and uncomfortable.

I would have rather had pimples. Mom wasn't much help regarding my sweat issues. She gave me my sister's deodorant, Secret. It smelled good for my sisters, but not on a man, and it wasn't an antiperspirant. I suffered as I was very naive in those days. I got a D in Mr. Garcia's Spanish class. It was my first D in school. I had to repeat Spanish the next year. It was quite a bit easier, and I had a better teacher, Mrs. Smith. I guess I learned something. I was a B student in high school. I took the college prep courses and sports were my salvation. I played on the "C" football team. It's for little guys like me. I loved football. That year I tried out for the "C" basketball team and was cut. Coach Ellis, our varsity football coach, coached "C" basketball. I did not like him for the rest of my life, and I don't hold grudges. I will show him. I substituted wrestling for basketball, and I made the JV team. I would wrestle in the 106-pound weight class. On the days of our wrestling matches, we would have to make weight since my normal weight was 110 pounds, I had to drop 4 pounds, depriving myself of food and water before matches. Mom hated that. My problem was that I would get so nervous before a match. I would be soaking wet. I did okay, I won some, and I lost some. The ones I won, were against bad wrestlers. At the end of the wrestling season, we had league finals. Our varsity wrestler, Richard Lake, did not make weight at 106 pounds. I had to wrestle varsity in his place. I was nervous. Guess what? I won; I was excited because that means I'm going to have another match. More nerves. My second match started and before I knew it, it was over. I got pinned in fifty-eight seconds! I made the footnotes. That was the quick pin of the tournament. I didn't go out for wrestling the next year. Christmas came around and my favorite gift was from my sister Pam. I unwrapped this small box to reveal its contents. It was "No Sweat Deodorant." I don't recall if it worked or if my sweat glands finally changed. Eventually, the problem did go away. I didn't use Secret from that day on. Thank you, Pam.

As I got older, I got more confident. I think sports were a big factor. I continued to play "C" football one more year and "B" football in my junior and senior years. I was thinking about going out for varsity, but Mr. Ellis was the coach, and I knew I would have sat on the bench. I made the right decision. By my senior year I weighed 145 pounds and a little under five foot seven. "B" football was great, and I loved it and I enjoyed my coach Mr. Fouts. I played middle linebacker on defense and left guard on offense. I enjoyed the contact and the activity at those positions. Rod Marinelli was the other middle linebacker. He eventually became an NFL coach for the Detroit Lions. Sister Pam and I visited Rosemead High and the city of Rosemead a few years ago. Rosemead converted from a mostly white and Hispanic community to mostly Asian community. I love Asian people and Asian food; in fact, my wife is Asian. After visiting our old town, we went to the high school for more nostalgia. It was after school hours and Asian kids were gathering at the various locations on campus. We went to our football stadium, and I noticed the name Rod Marinelli Stadium. Of course, I googled him right away and became aware of his accolades although I was a little jealous. I guess in retrospect it does make more sense to name a football stadium after a famous football coach than an entomologist, which I later became.

I was captain of our B team in my senior year because I had a good rapport with Coach Fouts. I wanted to be a running back. He allowed me, but I was not very good. I didn't have breakaway speed and I was not good at juking. Sometimes if a large blade of grass got in my way I would trip. Jimmy Cadam, one of my teammates for four years commented, "Can't you keep your balance?" Then to top it off, I later severely sprained my ankle. They didn't tape ankles in those days. My senior year in football was a disaster. In addition to football, because I got cut from basketball and got too nervous wrestling, I played tennis for three years. In my senior year, I made all-league honorable mention. I was more recognized because of my aggressiveness and joyful jubilation if I won. There were better players than me on our team who weren't mentioned. Doc McDonald was our number one player and the brother of my girlfriend, Debbie. Yes, I had a girlfriend during my junior and senior years. Bonnie, my twin sister, was not involved in sports but everything else. She was student body president, varsity cheerleader, princess, and queen. She was "poplar." At the end of the school year when we got our school yearbook, she would quickly go to the index and count the number of pages she was on. She would smash me. During our senior year, I was ASB Vice President under her, the ASB President. Pat and Pam were good examples for extra school activities, and we followed. The Bowman name was well recognized at Rosemead High School.

Girls in the '60s didn't participate in sports other than GAA (Girls Athletic Association). The GAA was very limited in scope, with the girls participating in field hockey, basketball, or softball. Prior to WW II, there were some schools allowing girls in varsity sports but after the war, girls varsity sports disappeared from high schools until Congress enacted Title IX, on June 23, 1972, which mandated that "No person in the United States shall, on the basis of sex be excluded from participation in, be denied of benefits of, or subjected to discrimination under any educational program or activity receiving Federal financial assistance." There was low participation in GAA in my high school days.

I had a lot of friends in high school. Most of my friends were through sports and other activities. In my junior and senior years, I only had two close friends.

Debbie McDonald was my high school girlfriend. She was a freshman, and I was a junior. She was a "B" football cheerleader, and I was a "B" football player. I knew Debbie before she got into high school but only in passing. I had been over to her house on several occasions to swim in their pool and hang around with Doc, her brother, and fellow tennis player. Their house was much bigger and much nicer than the average Rosemead house. Sometimes Debbie and her friend Colleen would be there. Debbie was smart, cute, and personable. She was in seventh or eighth grade at that time. By the time she entered Rosemead High School she had matured into an attractive, nicely figured freshman.

We hit it off and became boyfriend and girlfriend and eventually wore my ring. We were going steady. That is what we called it fifty-seven years ago. Debbie's only boyfriend before me was Paul McCartney of the Beatles. Debbie and I went to all the school activities together, varsity football games, dances, proms, and we even ate lunch together every school day. We were always together. Since I was with Debbie so much, I didn't have a lot of time for close friends other than through sports. In my senior year I broke up with Debbie. She took it hard. The breakup didn't last long, but when we got back together things weren't the same. Debbie was more cautious and protective because she didn't want to feel that hurt again. I was getting ready to go to college and she still had two more years of high school. Debbie decided to break up with me and my heart was broken.

My closest male friend in high school was Phil Day, although we had very little in common. He would often eat lunch with Debbie and me. If I went to his house, it was generally total boredom. He would work on his 1949 Chevy, and I would watch. He was very handy with tools and mechanics and that was not my interest. If he wasn't working on his Chevy, he was playing his Fender guitar. That wasn't my interest either. I did not like boredom; I had to always be busy like playing sports or doing something creative.

When I started college at Cal Poly, I abandoned my high school friends after joining Alpha Kappa Sigma fraternity. This became my new friend. I took Debbie to a few frat parties, but our relationship wasn't the same. Debbie was ready to make a change and although I wasn't, I had no other choice. I haven't seen Debbie since my freshman year in college. At times I wonder how she is doing if she has kids and what her life has become. I have always hoped for the best for her. Phil kept in touch by calling to wish me a happy birthday. I would see Phil and take him out to dinner when visiting my twin sister Bonnie. They lived a few miles apart. I would always pick up the tab because he never would. He had money too.

There was one friend from high school or even before high school that we reunited with many years later and re-established our friendship. His name was Gordon Wilson, affectionately known as "Big Gordy." He was three years older than me and almost a foot taller. He was close with my sisters Pat and Pam, especially Pam. He and Pam made a pact together; if they hadn't found a spouse by the time they were forty, they would marry each other. That didn't happen because they did find spouses before forty. I was an usher in "Big Gordy's" wedding; however, I have no recollection of it whatsoever and I wasn't drinking.

"Big Gordy" took me under his big wing. When he was a freshman or sophomore, he would come to visit Pat and Pam. They were "popular," a term so overused in the '60s and cool, and "hung out" which wasn't used in the '60s, with their Rosemead High School friends.

By my junior year, I got my driver's license. That was a fiasco. Mom took me to the California Department of Motor Vehicles. She made me nervous, and I failed my first driver's test. She was not sympathetic; she was mad. I passed on my second go-around but barely. I have never been a good driver. I blame it on my mother. Later in 1964, I bought my first car. It was a 1959 Volkswagen Beetle. I bought it from my parents for probably more than what it was worth. Nothing was free in those days. I paid $500 cash, from the money I saved from my paper route and summer jobs. That was equivalent to about $4,500 today. I don't recall if we looked up the Kelley Blue Book at the time, but if we did, I am sure I paid high blue book. I was still very happy because now I had my independence. I could drive to school instead of walking as I had done most school days.

These German-made Volkswagens were very common in those days because they were very economical. It had a 36-horsepower engine in the rear and was air-cooled. One of my friends had a 348 Chevy that put out 250 horsepower, but I was proud of my little car. It didn't have any bells and whistles; in fact, it didn't even have a gas gauge or a radio, but it did have a ten-gallon gas tank with a one-gallon spare. If you were to run out of gas, you could feel the engine chug. That was the time to turn on your spare tank. I could still go an additional thirty-five miles on the spare. In 1964, I could buy ten gallons of gas for $3 and my little VW Beetle would go approximately 350 to 370 miles on a tank of gas. The top speed was 75 mph if only one person was riding in the car. If there were two people, the maximum speed was 65 mph. If you came to a hill your speed would drop.

When you came to a large hill your speed would drop dramatically. Cal Poly, my future college, had a very large hill just before arriving at the campus. My top speed would drop to 35 mph as I reached its summit. Big semi-trucks would pass me as if I were standing still. I had sentimental value for this VW because it is the only car that I've ever owned. All the other cars I've driven have been company-owned.

CHAPTER 6

Family Vacations 1958–1963

My sisters were all Girl Scouts and Dad got involved with several of the Girl Scout fathers to build a Girl Scout camp in the San Gabriel Mountains. He would spend many weekends and work hard, but he loved it. I bet it reminded him of his days in the CCC. I would get to go occasionally. I remember one event when I was about eight years old. A small single-passenger airplane crashed near where several of us were playing. Tom Bender, Nancy's brother, who was several years older, and his friend, started running toward the crash. There were a lot of shrubs, bushes, and trees and I tried to run with them, but I couldn't keep up. I was six years younger, and I was crying as they were probably a couple of hundred yards ahead of me yelling for me to hurry. I finally got there to see my first dead person. That was a lot of fun. Thanks, Tom Bender. When I saw the dead body, I thought of my father because they were about the same age. I wondered if he had a little boy like me. As the ambulance came, we left the scene. During the day I kept reminiscing the sight of the dead pilot and thinking of my dad. I was wondering if the pilot had children, and if so, how tragic that would be.

Most of our experiences were pleasant. I loved the outdoors and nature. I loved anything that moved. Other memories from our family vacations include going over the Grapevine in our 1952 Ford, woody station wagon. The Grapevine is a section of road with a very steep incline for approximately six miles. Our car overheated and we had to pull off the side of the road. There wasn't much to the road edge, except a long way down, Mom would get very nervous. We had to let the car cool off and add water to the radiator. My dad was prepared for this; he had a water jug. We were not the only car to overheat, it was rather common in those days.

One of our favorite family summer vacations was at Twin Lakes, California in the Mammoth Mountain area near Bishop. I remember stopping at a bakery there that had the best sheepherder's bread. We stopped every year we went that way. Today it takes a little over five hours to get there from Rosemead but in those days I know it took over seven hours. Dad had built a camper top for a small utility trailer as he was very handy with woodworking. The curved camper top was rather ingenious and the sides folded out. We could store a lot of items such as canned goods, lanterns, cots, hammocks, sleeping bags, tents, fishing poles, and whatever.

When we were camping my parents were more relaxed. There was fishing, swimming, hiking, and playing with the other kids in the campground. Mom would relax and enjoy reading while Dad would always keep busy. He would pitch the tent, chop wood for the fire, and hike and fish. What I remember the most are the campfires after dark. We would roast marshmallows and sing songs such as "The Worms Crawl in and the Worms Crawl Out," "Head, Shoulders, Knees, and Toes," and "There Ain't no Flies on Us." These are a few that come to my mind. I am sure my sisters liked different songs. We all enjoyed Twin Lakes as every summer we would make so many friends. I know we went twice but we may have gone three times. One year we went to Yosemite and saw the giant Sequoias. For that trip, Dad bought a Volkswagen pick-up. The bed of the truck was covered with a sturdy canvas that went from the height of the cab to the back of the truck. It looked like a covered wagon. Actually, it was a covered Volkswagen. We didn't have to pull the trailer. If I am correct that VW pickup had a 36hp engine. It was slow trucking going through the mountains and we kids would always ask, are we almost there?

Our big trip was to Yellowstone National Park. Bonnie and I were the only kids to make that trip. I remember seeing Old Faithful, a grizzly bear, buffalo, antelope, and so many other animals. We were in pristine country, a lot different than Rosemead, a smoggy suburb of Los Angeles. I couldn't wait for our summer vacations. As we grew up and got into high school, we were preoccupied with our summer jobs and other things, and our summer vacations stopped. As we got older, Mom and Dad would go on vacations and not take us anymore.

We were teenagers and it wasn't cool to be with our parents. Looking back, I miss the family vacations. Why do teenagers go through an anti-parent stage? It seems universal.

CHAPTER 7

LA County Flood Control 1965–1969

It was the summer before my senior year at Rosemead, 1965, that I got a job with LA County Flood Control. My sister Pat was working there, and she heard that they were hiring summer help. I applied, and with Pat's help, I was hired. I initially worked in a lab, where we did soil compaction analysis. In LA County there can be extensive flooding if underground drainage is not allowed under the major roadways. It doesn't rain much in LA, but when it does, it can rain in bunches. Storm drains, culverts and flood channels all alleviate the flooding. When storm drains are put in, the soil is required to be compacted so the roads don't cave in. The soil would be tested by field soil testers to determine the compaction rate. Working in the lab, I would test various soils before the installation of the storm drains. I did gravity tests, moisture, compaction, and hydrometer tests to name a few. At the end of the summer, I felt quite proficient in the soils-lab. Civil Engineers would ask me questions and I could answer them. It was science, and I thoroughly enjoyed my summer work, but I missed being outdoors. Although smoggy, I enjoyed the outdoors more than the indoors.

My next summer my wish came true. To work as a soil tester, I had to take a county test to qualify for the position. I passed the exam and got a pay raise and a new title. I was now an official Jr. Engineering Aide and with that title, I got assigned to a field office to help in soil testing. I think I was making around $4.00 per hour. In 1967 the average median household income was $7,200. At $4.00 per hour, if I were working full-time, I would have made $8,320. My wages weren't shabby for summer work. I was still as frugal as ever. I saved whatever I could as I paid for my college and all my expenses. My job was to assist the Engineering Aides in doing soil compaction tests over the storm drains. The Engineering Aides were generally full-time employees and their test was harder than mine. Most of them made around $9,000 per year, and most of the Engineering Aides had some engineering in college and were quite proficient in math. Many had completed Jr. College or two years in college.

The storm drains were installed by contractors submitting bids for the work. The lowest bid gets the job. One contractor I remember most was Steve Slavovich and we called him Slobbering Steve because he slobbered. Wide and deep trenches were dug under roadways and the storm drains were connected. After connecting the pipes, the trenches would be backfilled with soil and compacted according to the soil lab's specifications. The soil would be watered down, then compacted using various heavy-duty equipment. When I first started, I was warned to watch out for the water trucks. Oops, I learned my lesson quickly as I got thoroughly soaked one day while in the trench.

The compactors would range in size from a one-man hand-held vibrating compactor to large heavy cylinders lifted by cranes above the soil and dropped over and over again. When working close to these compactors, you could feel the earth vibrating. The soil tester would take various tests to determine if the soil was compacted to its specifications. If all the soil tests passed, then the contractor could pave the road and get paid for his work. Some of the bigger storm drains were made of reinforced precast concrete pipes of up to 90" in diameter. The pipes were designed to fit into each other. The sections were roughly 10' long. Compaction tests were required at specified areas, distances, and various depths. We had several tests that we could take. I remember the sleeve test, ring, and sand-cone test. Once we got a test sample, we would weigh it and burn it. We had Coleman, gas-burning stoves on our trucks and would cook the soil, depleting it of all its moisture. Then we would re-weigh it and could determine its moisture content. There are many soil types from sand to loam to clay. Each soil will have a moisture rate that is ideal for compaction. If the ideal moisture is not obtained, then the soil tests could fail. The contractor putting in the storm drain would have to recompact the soil until proper compaction tests were achieved.

I worked with several different engineering aides in the field. I usually worked out of the El Monte field office. We had a civil engineer, Don, who would set our schedule and check our paperwork. He was a very nice, older, quiet man. Our soil testers, Engineering Aides, included Big Frank, Joe (Sonny), Keeny Van Horn, Junior, and Ron Welker, and about ½ dozen more that I can't remember their names. I worked with each one of them and my favorite was Keeny Van Horn. He was probably in his mid-forties and lean with blondish hair and a distinct mustache. He was a heavy smoker as were a lot of people of his generation. He was a hard and smart worker, consistent, reliable, very thorough and honest. He also was a great teacher, and very patient. Keeny taught me most of what I learned in soil testing. He made it very interesting.

In doing our various tests we had to perform a lot of calculations with a slide rule. For the younger generation, a slide rule is a mathematical tool. When in the right hands the slide rule could calculate a variety of mathematical problems. It was invented in the seventeenth century and was used until the pocket calculator came about in the early 1970s. This new pocket calculator was so much easier to use, and accurate. I never got to use the pocket calculator as a soil tester because I left LA County Flood Control before its invention. Keeny was very proficient with the slide rule and patiently tried to teach me. He was successful. On the other end of the spectrum of soil testers was Ron Welker. Ron was probably in his early fifties, rather good-looking with hair down to his shoulders. I hated working with him. He would drive from our base yard to the job site and park his truck and wouldn't get out to take the soil tests.

He would write up phony test results and wait for the contractor to come by with a little incentive, a bottle of Seagram's VO. Ron was generally inebriated by noon. He had a serious drinking problem, although on the outside he seemed very content. He was smart, charming, and drunk much of the time. Fortunately, I didn't have to work with him very often. I don't know how he was able to retain his job, but he did. I worked with approximately twelve different soil testers with various personalities. I learned something from them all. Working at LA County Flood Control was a great experience for me. I learned all about soil compaction but more than that, I learned how to work with a variety of people. I have tried to incorporate into my life the good I found in people. Keeney was a great example and Ron was a very poor example.

CHAPTER 8

Cal Poly 1966–1971

After I got through my freshman year in high school, I knuckled down as far as my studies. I took college prep courses but had no idea what I wanted to do or where I wanted to go to college. Fortunately, I had a very good counselor in Mrs. Smith. I never had to go to her before, because you generally don't have to see your counselor unless you are in trouble or failing. She interviewed me and looked at my grades. I told her that I wanted a job where I would be outdoors. She suggested Cal Poly Pomona which was about thirty minutes from our Temple City house and about thirty-five minutes for me and my VW. Yes, Temple City house. In my junior year of high school, my parents moved from Rosemead to Temple City. They moved to a much nicer house with a manicured dichondra lawn. A developer bought our Rosemead house and many other houses adjacent to the San Bernardino Freeway in Rosemead and built a Montgomery Ward shopping center.

Cal Poly

Cal Poly has a very spacious and spread-out campus. It has rolling hills with horses in its pastures. It was the home of the LA County Fairgrounds. At Cal Poly, as a freshman, we had to declare a major and I decided to study agronomy (soil sciences). With my job at LA County Flood Control, I was working with soils but more from an engineering perspective. Agronomy is associated with agriculture and doesn't require as much math. I was afraid of calculus. My classes were fun, and I learned how to study. It was the third quarter of my freshman year when I took a class in entomology, the study of insects. Dr. Jack Bath was probably in his late twenties at the time and came from the University of California at Riverside and taught the entomology class.

When he talked about insects, he would get so excited, and I would get excited. He realized how much I liked his course. Classes in entomology are not like classes in business (boring). There might have been fifteen students in the class, as most of the classes in our major were small. I loved his course, and in his lab, I saw my first cockroach. Living in Rosemead I never saw a cockroach. The climate is on the drier side and Mom was careful not to leave scraps of food around. Frank, a Chinese student from LA, brought in the specimen. We looked through our microscopes and keyed them out. We keyed them down to the species. This takes practice and knowledge about the external anatomy of insects. We determined the species to be *Blatta orientalis*, Oriental cockroach.

There are over 850,000 species of insects that have been identified. I can remember the Oriental roach easily because Frank was oriental. I got better and better in identifying insects to the point where I was good. I could remember things about insects so easily, even their long scientific names, it just came easy because I was infatuated with entomology. Even today, I can still remember long Latin scientific names that I haven't used for fifty years. I have a hard time remembering my grandchildren's names. As you may remember my dad called us all honey and I was no honey, I got a D in my first Spanish class, but I can remember Latin?

Dr. Bath and I became close; he confided in me. He told me that he went through a nervous breakdown in trying to decide what major he was going to choose for college. He was debating entomology or Egyptian anthropology. I changed my major from agronomy to entomology because of him. By choosing entomology he changed my life; he made it so exciting. The last time I looked, Dr. Bath was still teaching at Cal Poly. He must be in his eighties and I bet he still gets excited about insects as I do. My new major became Agricultural Biology - Economic Entomology. I didn't know what I was going to do, but who does as a freshman in college? My brother-in-law, who rose to the top rank with the LA County Sheriff's Department, thought I had lost my marbles. Cal Poly was a great school with its main emphasis on learning by doing, not just by reading. In my Bee science class, we had our own hives and we maintained them. In my structural pest control class, I worked with a pest control company in Pomona, and I learned how to inspect homes for termites and how to treat them. I also went out with a pest control company and learned pest treatments and I went to farms in the vicinity and learned their various pest control techniques.

There was still a lot of book learning. I took quite a bit of chemistry, the hardest one was organic chemistry. I remember our instructor, Dr. Vladimir Putin, or something like that. He was Russian and very stoic, and would write organic formulas on the chalkboard, yes, we had chalkboards in those days, faster than we could copy them down. We went through the whole organic chemistry book in ten weeks. It was a very hard course, but I studied, and I did well. I got a C. I know it was a C+ bordering B-, but he only gave out A, B, C, D, or Fs. I learned quite a bit. It was a very tough class and I studied and studied. I took classes on pest control procedures, including pest control chemicals; many of the pesticides are organic compounds. Organic chemistry helped. The hardest and worst class that I took was British Literature. It was my senior year and I needed one more English class to graduate. I didn't know it, but that class was for students majoring in English. I had no previous knowledge of literature, let alone British Literature. I hated it and struggled. I got a D in that class, probably closer to a D minus. It was my only D in college. I guess I was better at Latin than old English.

In my Bee Science class, I had a very humbling experience. Our instructor, Dr. Hobbs, had a mild heart attack while we were taking his course. We were assigned to the Cal Poly beekeeper, Don. He had worked with the bees at Cal Poly for several years. He had many beehives, and the bees would pollinate nearly everything in their vicinity. On this particular day, we were going to check our hives and extract honey. We would normally wear our white bee suits with gloves and our veil. The bee suit and gloves were awkward, and it was hard to see through the veil. Don told me that most beekeepers don't wear bee suits. He also mentioned that experienced beekeepers take stings and become immune to their pain. He convinced me. This afternoon I chose not to wear my bee suit, gloves, or veil. The other students thought I was just showing off.

The initial procedure is to remove the hive cover and shake it down to remove the bees. As I put my hand over the hive cover a bee stung me. I expected at least that. When I shook the hive cover down the bees came straight for my black wooly socks. In seconds I probably took close to 100 stings. I was mortified and humbled as I left the site in extreme pain and I sang a song as I quickly left, Uh, ah o ah ah. By the next day, my ankles swelled up to the size of large grapefruits. What did I learn in this class? I learned I would never trust Don again and I would not wear black wooly socks to work with bees. Bees do not like black wooly socks because it reminds them of a black woolly bear, and so much for hands-on learning. I guess I learned the hard way from it. The day after my bee-stinging event, I had a test in that class, and I aced it in pain and agony.

Cal Poly was on the quarter system. Each quarter usually lasted ten to eleven weeks. On the quarter system, you will take about 1/3 more classes than on the semester system. It seemed like some of the instructors tried to jam a semester into a quarter, like my organic chemistry course. The quarter system also allowed us to take a lot of classes. I took an art sculpture class where I made a bronze figurine that weighed almost twenty pounds. We had to provide our own metals to make the bronze. I raided my dad's garage and I had to go to the junkyard and buy some scrap copper. Our instructor provided the wax. I think he got it from Don the beekeeper. With various knives and scalpels, we carved our image out of the wax. My image was a pregnant nude lady sitting with her knees up and her hands holding her head. Once she was carved, I added vents and a funnel of wax. Then I coated her with a high heat resistant plaster, which I brushed on. I put her in a wooden box and poured another type of plaster on my sculpture. Then she was placed in the oven to allow the wax to melt away. Now I have a big chunk of plaster approximately one foot square with a hollow image of my lady inside. I could finally pour the bronze but first I had to melt it.

Bronze melts at 1675 degrees Fahrenheit. We had a propane gas-fired crucible furnace to do that job. The bronze is poured into the funnel made of wax that is no longer there. The bronze fills all the voids and air comes out of the vents. Now you have a bronze funnel connected to her (okole) rear end and vents protruding from her body. It is time to cut off all those extraneous things. Then I took a file to smooth all the cut areas. Almost done. I decided to patina my lady by wrapping her in rags soaked in ammonia. This created a chemical process and she turned slightly green. This sculpture's wax process dates from the third millennium BC with few changes. Today my lady is a doorstop in our downstairs living area. We made three other sculptures in that class. The only one I remembered is the clay sculpture of an old man's head. That one wasn't good enough to be a doorstop.

Another class I enjoyed was Equestrian. We rode on English saddle which were for the prim and proper. On the other hand, a western saddle or I call a cowboy saddle, certainly was not prim and proper. We had to learn all the proper techniques for mounting the horse, riding, and dismounting. We learned how to properly walk, trot, gallop, and run our horses, prim and properly and we also fed and groomed our horses. There was a cute girl in our class whom I had a crush on. She was small and yet well endowed. Her hair was always perfect with never a strand out of place. When she rode, her well endowment moved up and down and not always at the same pace and her hair did not move at all. I liked riding with her. I was disappointed when I found out that she had a boyfriend, but that didn't keep me from riding with her.

Another hands-on class I took as a freshman when I was studying Agronomy, was my tractors class. We didn't just study about tractors, we drove them. We learned how to back them up with two trailers attached. That was quite a feat. My mom wasn't with me, so I did better. I graduated from Cal Poly with a 3.14 GPA. I got almost all As in the classes in my major and mostly Bs and a few Cs and one D in British Literature. I would give Cal Poly very high marks as an excellent University. I certainly enjoyed it.

Fraternity Life

After my freshman year, I joined a fraternity. At that time Cal Poly was certainly not considered a party school. There were about five fraternities and maybe three sororities. When I pledged, I think we had six active members in our fraternity. The fraternity had been on the decline for several years. Our pledge class consisted of four new prospects, Derek Foster, Atilla McKrenzy, George Kornhoff, and me. Derek was studying aerospace engineering, Attila and George started at engineering but changed their majors. I was the only Aggie. Cal Poly has a great engineering department, and it is hard. As pledges, we had a lot of fun together. One time George and I decided to go to this massage parlor in Pomona that offered full-body massages. When we finished, I was fully relaxed and satisfied but George told me he was relaxed and unsatisfied. I said, "Did you ask for a full body massage?" His reply? "No." It takes an Aggie because Aggies know about the birds and the bees.

Alpha Kappa Sigma was our fraternity, and we pledges knew it as Alpha Kappa Sigma, Sir! as we stood at attention before one of the active members. My Big Brother was John Herr who became a close friend. We had some harassment, but it wasn't overt. We four pledges were taken to the San Gabriel Mountains blindfolded at night with no transportation back. That was an experience that I have forgotten about, but I must have reached home. All four of us got accepted into the Fraternity and we all became close friends until I became the housemother. I moved from our Temple City house to live in the fraternity house in 1967. I think that was Mom's happiest day in her life, but she didn't offer to pay even a part of my rent or tuition. I think my rent for a room at the frat house was $75 per month. George and Derek were already living there. I was appointed housemother by Steve Scherer, our President. What a thankless job. Both Derek and George were slobs and they never listened to my requests. If Mom had those two slobs as her sons, she would have realized just how near-perfect I was.

As typical in a fraternity we had parties, drinking beer and other healthy alcoholic beverages, and some smoked a little weed, but weed was taboo in the house. Mostly we were quite civil and a pretty good bunch of guys. The next two pledge classes were good-sized, so the fraternity grew. One of my best friends was Kip Cox who pledged after I did. We decided to get an apartment in our senior year and move out of the frat house. It was a very good move. I enjoyed Kip and his friendship and we shared a nice clean apartment. Derek still lived in the frat house, and we called his room, "the doghouse." Kip was a good-looking guy. If you didn't know him well you would think he was conceited, but he wasn't. He was sometimes a little indifferent but when you get to know Kip, you'll realize you have met a great person. I think we shared the apartment for about one year.

In my senior year, I was anxious to graduate and move on. My experience at Cal Poly for the most part was super. I got an excellent education and met some great guys and a few girls. I made a good choice.

CHAPTER 9

Uncle Sam; My New Boss 1969–1975

In 1969 I was finishing my junior year in college; The Vietnam War was in full force. Vietnam was colonized by the French in the late 1900s and got its independence after a victory in the First Indochina War in 1954. Then Vietnam was divided into two countries, North Vietnam and South Vietnam. Bitter conflicts resulted between the two countries. Ho Chi Minh, the leader of the North, a communist, invaded the non-communist South. Russia and China were in support of the communists. The United States entered the war on November 1, 1954, as anticommunists, and pro-democracy. By the late '60s, the war was causing division in our country. Why were we fighting in Vietnam? It was termed the "domino effect." Communism was taking hold in many countries with one country and another would fall to a communistic form of government. We were concerned that if South Vietnam became communist then Cambodia, Laos, Thailand, etc. might also fall like dominos.

There was a lot of disenchantment among the United States populous regarding our involvement in Vietnam. Some Americans were in favor of the war, and many were against it. As the death toll rose, more and more were against it. Name-calling was common. You pinko, you commie lover, you pacifist, you hawk, you war-mongering idiot, were common expressions during this time. War protests were ongoing with flag-waving, sign-holders protesting the war, and sign holders protesting the sign holders. The majority of protests were on college campuses. The student strike in 1970 was a massive protest across most campuses in the United States, including Cal Poly. A major university protest occurred on 5/4/1970 at the campus of Kent State University. There the National Guard was called in to quell the protests at a peace rally opposing the expansion of the Vietnam War into Cambodia. As the protest got heated up, guardsmen shot and killed four students and injured many.

Many other schools had major antiwar protests during this time as a result of what happened at Kent State and Vietnam, Lyndon Johnson's approval rating was at an all-time low. He declared he would not run for a second term. The war began in 1954 and was at its peak in 1968 when over 500,000 US troops were deployed. The death toll was estimated to be over 1.3 million. Almost ½ were civilians. I wasn't an avid protester at that time because I had mixed feelings, but more and more I was turning against the war. After the data came out, especially regarding civilian deaths, I was against the war. I did not want to go to Vietnam and fight in a political war.

As I write this, the US currently has an all-volunteer army, but when I was twenty-one years old, it wasn't all-volunteer; there was a draft in place. Even if you didn't want to join the military you were required to if you were drafted. The draft was based on a lottery system, 366 birthdates were randomly selected to determine who would most likely have to serve in the Army. The lower your draft number the more likely you would be called to serve in the military. My draft number was relatively low, but while in college I was draft deferred, meaning that I was eligible for the draft once I graduated from college. I had to make a choice. I had one year left of my college deferment. I could leave the country and live in Canada and lose my citizenship as many did, or I could burn my draft card, which would probably end with me in jail, or I could become a conscientious objector and join some obscure religion that resisted war or I could develop a medical deferment such as blindness or I could get a bone spur.

I chose to join the National Guard. By joining the National Guard, I was much less likely to go to Vietnam and fight in a war that I didn't support. By joining the National Guard, I was volunteering for a six-year enlistment. I was required to attend Basic Training and Advanced Individual Training (AIT). I was going to learn how to fire big cannons and become a cannoneer. Very useful knowledge to make me a better human. My basic training was in Fort Campbell, Kentucky and it was hot and muggy. California weather is relatively dry, and I was not used to the humidity. In basic training, you must get used to it. I rather enjoyed the training.

It was hard and it reminded me of "Hell Week" in football. It is designed to be highly intense and challenging. Basic training is also intended to play with the young minds of the recruits. I am somewhat of a masochist and very competitive, so I made it fun. I had a great drill sergeant who was Black and was the first Black person whom I had an acquaintance with. He was very neat and precise. As we marched in unison, he would call the cadence to our footsteps as we would call back with a cadence song such as "Is Jody Stealing Your Wife, oh oh." He was calm and in control and rather quiet but didn't mingle with the troops. He was a sergeant, and we were lowly privates. If I were on the battlefield, I would like to have him in my squad. Our sergeant major had a different personality. He was a big man of Hawaiian ancestry. We didn't see him often and that was good because he scared me.

After graduating from basic training, we privates boarded military planes to go to our next assignment. My AIT was in Fort Sill, Oklahoma. There I was to learn various duties dealing with 105mm and 155mm howitzers. These are big cannons, but the military describes them as light field howitzers. The shell of the 105mm weighs 15.1 kg. That didn't help me either. In 1975, Congress passed the Metric Conversion Act. The US was going to change to the metric system, but when? It never happened. I did the conversion. The projectile weighed 33.29 pounds, and the circumference at the base is 4.134 inches. The 155mm weighs 95 pounds and the circumference is 6.06 inches. The 105 Howitzer has a range of 7 miles and the 155 a range of 9 miles. They both are very accurate and both these howitzers were successfully used in WWII. We learned all about these weapons in the field and in the classroom. I think we spent sixteen weeks and I hardly remember a thing and I hardly want to.

After graduating from AIT, I went back to California where I could finish college. College was still waiting for me as the Vietnam War was still dragging on. Now my assignment was different, I have five and a half more years of military service. We were required to serve one weekend per month and then two weeks during the summer. I disliked almost every minute of it. It was the worst job I ever had except for my job at a carwash being in a tire well washing tires, as I was soaking wet. I quit the first day of that job, but I couldn't quit the military. I dreaded the National Guard weekends. Longer hair was in style for men during my time in service. We had to report to duty with a proper haircut. I wore a wig, which was allowed as did most of my fellow servicemen. It was a short-haired wig to cover our long hair. What a pain in the butt.

Now I am a military veteran. I realize the need for a strong military, but it is hard to justify the fact that the US military budget in 2018 was approximately $649 billion. When you compare our budget to other powerful countries such as China $250 billion, France $64 billion, Russia $61 billion, Germany $50 billion, Japan $47 billion, and Canada $21.6 billion, one can see that our budget appears excessive. In fact, in 2020 the United States spent more money on defense than the next ten countries with the largest defense budgets combined. In addition, we are a major arms supplier throughout the world. I just feel there needs to be a much better approach for a peaceful world. Can't a portion of that money be spent on mental illness and mental evaluations for our politicians?

CHAPTER 10

My Start at NAMCO 1971

I graduated from Cal Poly in December of 1970 and was relieved, due to burnout and a desire to move forward. After the holidays were over, I began looking for my first real job. I had several options, but I had no idea what was available. I could go to the State and apply to become an agricultural inspector. That work didn't appeal to me. One of the first interviews I had was with Neil A. McClain Company, which did soil fumigation for strawberries and sold and distributed pest control chemicals. I was told that if I were hired, I would be provided with a new car and my job would be to sell and distribute pest control chemicals. I was pleased with the pay and the benefits they offered. My VW had over 100,000 miles and was almost totally worn out. The person who interviewed me was Walt Estelle and I liked him right off the bat. He oversaw the sales staff of the office. After the interview, I was quite confident I would get the job. I followed a few more leads, but they didn't appeal to me.

Then on February 9, 1971, in the early morning hours, the San Fernando earthquake occurred. I was living in Pomona, approximately fifty miles from the epicenter, and woke up to my apartment shaking and rumbling. Kip had a thirty-gallon fish tank in the living room with water splashing over its side. I was lucky, there was no noticeable damage. However, the closer you got to San Fernando, the damage was much more visible. This quake caused over $500 million in damage in addition, it also created a lot of concern for aftershocks and the possibility of future quakes along the San Andreas fault. Southern Californians were on pins and needles.

Approximately two weeks had passed since I had my interview with Neil A. McClean Co. I was eager to hear back from them but had received no word. I decided to call and asked to speak to Walt Estelle. Walt wasn't in so the switchboard gave me to Milt Cole, Walt's boss. I asked Milt "What is my status?" His reply, "You have no status." This broke my ego, in retrospect, I realize I could have phrased my question a little better. I did get a call a few days later from Walt, offering me the job. He explained that there were delays due to the earthquake. My ego was restored.

Neil A. McClean Co. soon became NAMCO after my start. Two brothers, Neil McClean and Hugh McClean, originally from Australia, sold their interests in the company as I entered the scene. The company consisted of two different divisions. They provided a service to the strawberry growers in California soil fumigation, and they sold pest control chemicals and products to the pest control industry. I wasn't involved in soil fumigation. Hugh McClean had a big part in the development of this section of the company as he designed the injection method and delivery system for the fumigant to go into the soil. A tractor with a fumigant, fumigant injectors, and a 20' roll of 6 mil polyethylene would be driven over the unplanted strawberry fields. As the tractor moved forward a combination of methyl bromide and chloropicrin fumigants would be injected into the soil and then covered with polyethylene as the tractor moved forward. The fumigants were injected to kill nematodes and other plant pathogens. This method started in the 1960s and is still being used today.

I worked in the other division, pest control chemicals, and product sales. I was hired to take over sales in a large area in Southern California. I was trained by Henry Zepeda who was leaving his territory to me so he could better serve the Arizona market for NAMCO. I have never met a person who could talk as fast as Henry and when he explained something, he would get excited in a good way. I liked Henry, he was a fellow Cal Poly graduate as were most of the employees of NAMCO, and he was fun to work with.

I loved what I was doing. At Cal Poly I had classes that prepared me for this job. My major, Economic Entomology dealt with nearly everything I was about to do including the study of insects and other economic pests and control measures including biological control, pesticide control, and mechanical control, such as trapping and baiting. A little side note: We just celebrated my seventy-third birthday party at our home and quite a few guests were invited. Food tables were set up and

Jennifer said, "What should we do, flies are getting on the food?" As a profound Economic Entomologist, I didn't answer. About three minutes later, Evelyn brought out a fan. I have taught her well. This is a simple form of mechanical control and it worked.

In my sales area, there were probably 200 Pest Control Operators (PCOs) businesses, some nurseries, some large landscape companies, and various other businesses that bought pest control products. Our business was well established. I added some new accounts; however, the majority of my accounts had purchased from us before I started. My job was mostly public relations, introducing new products and providing information on how our products are used. In addition, I taught classes on Entomology. Before the beginning of my new job on December 2, 1970, the EPA (Environmental Protection Agency) was authorized by Congress and formed under the Nixon administration. It has been over fifty years since its origin. In 2020 the EPA had 13,758 employees and an annual budget of $9,057,401,000 (Wikipedia). EPA had a significant impact on our industry. We were in for a big change.

Why was the EPA formed? The environmental movement was very substantial by the close of the 1960s. Rachael Carson wrote a dynamic book, *Silent Spring*, which was published on September 27, 1962. Her book generated a great awareness about the indiscriminate use of pesticides. There was a lot of resistance to this environmental movement. I remember in our industry, mostly the old-timers were opposed to change. On the front cover of a pest control magazine, was a picture of an elderly, thin man, Fred Loybal, sitting with his wife standing behind him. Fred was one of my customers. His hand was held open exposing the DDT capsule with a glass of water in the other hand. In the picture, he was implying that he was going to take the DDT orally to show it was safe for humans. When the industry saw this pest control magazine cover, many were very concerned because Fred had a drinking problem, and it wasn't water and DDT.

DDT was used at the end of WWII as an effective insecticide against insect-borne diseases including malaria, typhus, and body lice. The mosquito was the main target; however, it was very effective against most insects and arthropods. This effective new treatment for the mosquito causing malaria and typhus was called a miracle. Deaths from these diseases declined dramatically due to the effects of DDT. DDT was the first of the modern synthetic insecticides. Before DDT, chemicals such as arsenic, strychnine, mercury, and copper sulfate were in use. In addition, some insecticides made from plants were used, such as nicotine, from tobacco, pyrethrum from African daisies, and rotenone, from derris root. DDT initially proved to be a superior insecticide. It was synthetic and was classified as a chlorinated hydrocarbon. It did not break down easily, the human toxicity was relatively low, and it was affordable.

DDT was applied in a multitude of methods. Airplanes loaded with DDT were flown over mosquito-infested areas and eventually, our crops were sprayed and dusted. The more it was used, insects developed higher resistance. Greater concentrations of DDT were required to kill the insects resulting in even greater use. DDT was applied by vehicle-driven foggers in cities and counties in an indiscriminate manner targeting mosquitos. Kids were often seen chasing the fogger trucks and playing in the DDT mist. It was applied in and around our homes for cockroaches and ants as a general insecticide by pest control operators and do-it-yourselfers. It was applied directly to the bodies of lice-infested soldiers and prisoners. It was applied in our schools and our forests. It could be applied as a liquid, a granular, a fog, and dust. It was applied nearly everywhere insects existed. What we learned about DDT came about largely because of Rachael Carson's, *Silent Spring.* One of the side effects of using DDT was the effect it had on non-target organisms such as beneficial insects, birds, and mammals. We almost lost our national symbol, the bald eagle, mostly due to the overuse of DDT. In 1963 their population count was 417 nesting pairs in the lower United States. As of February 10, 2021, there were 9,700 nesting pairs in the lower US. Many other bird populations were severely affected. It was later determined that eggshells were affected by DDT. The eggshells were thinning by the overuse of this miracle pesticide causing the eggs to crack prematurely.

Why was DDT so effective and what happened? DDT was a very stable molecule and had very effective insecticidal properties. When it was introduced, there was no resistance, but as nature adapts resistance began. The more it was used the more the resistance. DDT was used in the United States for almost three decades and is still used in certain parts of the world, including India, Africa, and North Korea. I feel that the EPA made the correct decision in banning the use of

DDT in that Malaria was eradicated from the US in the early 1950s and Typhus is very rare. DDT had done a great job. In doing a great job, it also caused a lot of harm to the environment. We overused it, we abused it, and now we need to learn from our experience.

CHAPTER 11

Moving to Hawaii 1971–1976

My job was a continual learning experience. The more I learned, the more confident I became. I worked in the El Monte office for six months when I got a call from the Vice President of the company, Norm Ehmann. I had only briefly met him because he worked out of our Milpitas office. Norm was a large man, on the heavy side with a large nose. He was probably in his sixties and had been with Neil A. McClean company for over twenty years. He was well educated and smart. He graduated from UCLA with a bachelor's degree in chemistry. He was a Board-Certified Entomologist, had a master's degree in public health, and he was a Registered Sanitarian. Norm flew down from San Francisco to meet me. Why? I had no idea. I quickly found out that it was regarding a new job assignment.

Jim Booth, our Hawaii representative, had been electrocuted while working on the greenhouse he was building. Norm told me of this sad situation and asked if I would be the NAMCO rep. in Hawaii. I had never lived out of the Los Angeles area in my twenty-three years except for my time in the National Guard. What an opportunity, it took me two seconds to say yes. I had one concern, my roommate Kip and I was renting an apartment together so when I got home, I told Kip that I was going to work in Hawaii and asked him if he wanted to join me. He agreed. We arranged to ship our furniture, personal belongings including two motorcycles, and whatever little we had at the time. I was glad that Kip was joining me on my new journey. He was my best friend, a frat brother, and he was a lot of fun.

Kip stayed back for about two weeks to get our furniture and personal belongings to the dock. I joined my new boss, Norm Ehmann, to fly to Hawaii. Wow! That was a long flight. The longest flight that I had before Hawaii was to

Fort Campbell, Kentucky. It was September 1971, and it was warm and humid. Coming from California, I was used to the heat but not the humidity. We went to the office to meet my staff of one employee, Kay Tamura. Kay was around fifty years old and an attractive Japanese lady. She had one daughter who was about my age. When Norm introduced me to Kay it appeared that her heart just sank. She said, "You're so young." I was twenty-three but probably looked twenty. I know she was initially disappointed. I was her new boss, and she was going to teach me. At times she seemed rather reluctant but overall, she did a great job. As our inside salesperson, she was very organized and a pro at what she did, as almost all the sales came over the phone. She managed the inventory and took care of almost all the paperwork. Remember, this is before computers and scanners. Everything was manual; however, she had an electric typewriter and a calculator.

My job was to call on customers, deliver products, keep our inventory in order and keep our customers happy. I had to drive a forklift, which we shared with our co-tenant of the warehouse. Our inventory took up approximately 1,500 square feet, so we didn't require a lot of space. The smaller items were on racks on pallets. Most of our inventory was in 55, 30, and 5-gallon drums and 200-pound cylinders. The majority of chemicals that I was selling in 1971 have since been banned. We sold many of the chemicals that were discussed in Rachael Carson's book, *Silent Spring*. The pest control industry used these chemicals in a much more sparing way than the agriculture Industry. However, this did not justify their use. The chemicals belonging to the chlorinated hydrocarbons were widely used in treating under foundations for subterranean termites, for long-lasting residual treatment. They were also used in and around the perimeter of houses and businesses for general pest control. This classification of chemicals included DDT. Just before my joining NAMCO in 1971, DDT lost its registration to be used in and around homes. The majority of alternates were other chlorinated hydrocarbons, just as bad or worse than DDT. They included Aldrin, Dieldrin, Lindane, Heptachlor, and Chlordane. A 55-gallon drum of Chlordane weighed over 600 pounds. We supplied Vikane, the fumigant used by the industry to fumigate drywood termites in homes and structures. Vikane came in cylinders of 125 pounds of gas with the tare weight of about 75 pounds. A full cylinder of Vikane weighed around 200 pounds. Drywood termites are found in warmer climates with mild winters such as Florida, southern Texas, Southern California, and Hawaii and they are by far worst in Hawaii.

The major indoor pest problem in Hawaii in the '70s was German cockroaches and ants. In so many cases the German cockroach infestations were almost unbelievable, a time before cockroach baits became popular. Chlordane was used as a perimeter spray and was very effective against ants. Diazinon and Dursban were the two most widely used pesticides in Hawaii for interior cockroach treatment. It was my job to know the market, to know the chemicals, and to know my customers and keep them well supplied with chemicals, products, and current information. We had token competition. C. Brewer, one of the Hawaii Big Five, a conglomerate, sold some, but we had the majority of the market. We were specialized in supplying this niche market.

Kay had done a super job in retaining our market share. Norm was at my side to begin learning the Hawaii market. One of the first things we did was to find a condo to live in. Norm could get things done fast. We found a condo that first day; I think it was the only one we saw. I don't remember the name of the condo, but I do recall the condo manager. His name is Mr. Ruley. Remember, this was fifty years ago. I re-met Mr. Ruley at Alaeloa in Napili, Maui about thirty years later, as he was the resident manager there. The condo we rented was fine; however, it wouldn't be my first choice if I had to do it over again. We should have been closer to the University of Hawaii. With Kip and I in our young twenties and just out of college, it seemed as if we were living at an old-age home. Well, it would do for six months, because that was the length of my lease.

Norm took me out to meet my customers. I didn't have a language barrier in California, but in Hawaii I did. The majority of my clients were locals and that could mean anything from Hawaiian/Chinese, Portuguese/Japanese, Puerto Rican/Korean, Filipino/Japanese, or any combination of Hawaiian, Chinese, Japanese, Portuguese, Filipino, Korean, and Puerto Ricans. Locals didn't consider white people (haoles) as locals. Haoles were haoles. These ethnic groups made up the Hawaii sugar workers. Except for the Hawaiians, these workers were brought to the Hawaiian Islands from their various countries to provide the hard labor for the sugar cane plantations. The managers of the plantations were nearly all White, and many were related to the early Hawaiian missionaries. The sugar workers lived in plantation camps in substandard termite-eaten structures. By living all together, they developed their own language and expressions. This language was termed Pidgin English.

A few of my favorite Pidgin-English expressions are: "Oh, that kaukau so ono, it broke da mout." That food is so delicious. Or "Hey, brah, don't give me stink eye." Don't give me a dirty look. "You stay pau hana?" Are you through with work? "Hey brah, I gotta go shishi." I have to go pee. "You got da kine?" Do you have anything? Usually, something or da kine will come out like "Do you have da kine, you know da kine, da kine dog? Oh yea, I got da kine, Lucky, my dog. "Hey Brah, your kids have hanabata." Hanabata is the snot that is wet or dries under your nostrils. The locals often refer to the hanabata days as your childhood days. Hana in Japanese means nose and bata in Pidgin English is butter, like pass the bata. So hanabata in Pidgin is nose butter.

When I started selling chemicals and products to my customers, I had a hard time understanding the locals. In the '70s Pidgin English was very prevalent and if you were local and you didn't speak Pidgin you weren't "Dakine." I wasn't local and I was "one haole." Haole in Hawaiian can have several meanings; not native Hawaiian, of European descent, Caucasian, and stranger, are common meanings. However, when I got to Hawaii in the early'70s, Haole was a Caucasian. There was some prejudice against the Haoles as well there should have been. In the sugar and pineapple plantation days, the big bosses of the plantations were generally Haoles. Some were mean and demeaning to their plantation workers. As the plantation camps started breaking up in the '50s and '60s and their school system started integrating into the state-run schools, the Haoles were a minority and at times there were conflicts.

I remember hearing about the "Hate Haole Days." I didn't see much of it and sometimes it was deserved because the Haoles didn't show respect as they should have for the locals. I loved the locals from the beginning. I am fortunate because I didn't have built-in prejudices because of my upbringing. Growing up in Rosemead, we had a variety of different ethnic groups. We had a few Asians; our ASB President was Rick Yamamoto, and his sister, Jane, was in my freshman English class. The majority of students were Caucasian, then Mexican American, German, Italian, Spanish, Hawaiians, but we had no Blacks in our school. On the whole, we got along well. In Hawaii, I fit in. I loved the local people, but I just couldn't understand them. That was short-lived. I was determined to learn Pidgin English. I was told about Kent Bowman, my last name's sake—alias K. K. Ka'umanua.

He was born in Hilo and was an ethnic blend of French, Hawaiian, Scottish, and English. Although he had some Hawaiian blood, he looked Haole. He was "one haole," with the name, cow manure. He was a comedian, recording artist, businessman, and actor in the Hawaii Five-0. series. He recorded stories in Pidgin-English and they were available on 33 1/3 rpm records*. His stories were generally well-known nursery rhymes. Some of the titles include "Goldie the Blond Malihini and the Three Wild Pua's," ("Goldilocks and the Three Bears"), "Rumple Dakin Skin," ("Rumplestiltskin"), "Little Lei Puahi," ("Little Red Riding hood"), "Keaka and the Beanstalk," ("Jack and the Beanstalk"). In a short period, I had purchased three record albums and listened to them, not once, not twice but probably close to twenty times. After doing my fairy tale homework, I was somewhat proficient in Pidgin English. I was intrigued by it. I learned to understand and speak Pidgin, but haloes sound stupid when speaking Pidgin to a local so I only spoke Pidgin to other haoles. *(For my grandchildren, these records were about the size of a dinner plate. They were played on a record player. Today you can go to your iPhone and type in Kent Bowman and you can listen to the same recordings I did fifty years ago. Try it, you'll like it.)

I enjoyed meeting my new customers with Norm who was a gregarious, intense, energetic man. He was very highly respected in the industry. He was one of the hardest-working individuals I have ever met. We called on our Oahu customers, then went to the outer islands. We spent two days on Kauai, two on Maui, and two on the Big Island. What an experience. I loved what I was doing and seeing beautiful people, and the beautiful islands. The customers, on the whole, seemed very nice and appreciative of our service. It was different from California. There I didn't get that same feeling. Here in Hawaii, I learned the term, "Aloha" and it was sincere. Almost everyone showed concern for the family of Jim Booth and showed concern for this new, young "haole boy."

Norm left after our outer island trip, leaving Kay and me in Hawaii. I soon realized how much work I had to do. Kay had written up a lot of orders that needed delivery as soon as I got back, and I was the delivery boy. I had to learn how to get the chemicals out of the warehouse and onto the truck and then to the customer. My truck was a 1969 blue Chevy pickup with a winch for loading the big items. When the winch lifted a 600-pound drum of Chlordane it appeared the truck would break, but it didn't. Once loaded up, I had to get to my location. That was no simple task for a person who has a tough time reading a map unless it was oriented toward true North. The roads in Honolulu are very chaotic and the names of the roads are Hawaiian, like Kalanianaole Hwy., Kalaunu Ave., or Kalakaua Ave. Traveling in a new city with windy roads, all named with Hawaiian names, and congested traffic was a big challenge with no (GPS). I am almost sure Kay thought I was drinking between deliveries, I was sweating.

My blue Chevy truck had no air-conditioning or wind wings. It was September and hot and muggy. Very muggy in fact. I was used to my air-conditioned Ford Torino back in El Monte. The hottest time of year was ending and changing to, hot and muggy then warm and muggy and by December it was just right, and it would stay just right for seven months. The roads were becoming a little more familiar and I managed my way through the challenges. The easiest part for me was dealing with the customers and knowing my product line. I was good at that. My customers liked me, and I liked them. I got involved in the Hawaii Pest Control Association as an avid member and taught various classes to the association members and my job became my life. I loved it.

There was a sales meeting in San Jose, California in March 1972. I was going to fly down to see my family in southern California after the sales meeting. Much to my surprise at the sales meeting, I was honored with, the "Salesman of the Year" award. I was shocked. I didn't know I was in contention. Norm liked me. There were about thirty salespeople in NAMCO at the time. I call it beginner's luck. Kay had so much to do with my initial success, but I was the one recognized and not her. I threw heaps of praise on her when I returned to Hawaii.

A very memorable event occurred in my first few months while living in Hawaii; however, some of it is foggy. When I first arrived, Hawaii was in the midst of a shipping strike that began on July 1, 1971. The longshoremen were requesting a pay raise, more job security, and better benefits. Mechanization of the shipping industry was taking hold from bulk cargo to containerization. Containerization was much more efficient and required much less manpower. The two sides, International Labors and Warehouse Union (ILWU) and the Pacific Maritime Association (PMA) were far apart in their negotiations. About 15,000 longshoremen were striking on the West Coast, Alaska, and Hawaii. Hawaii, being the most isolated landmass in the world, is nearly entirely dependent on shipping. How were we going to get our supplies? Or were we going to get our supplies? This strike had major consequences.

Sugar from Hawaii is refined in California and could not be shipped as well as pineapple. Warehouses were being stored to their maximum. Eventually, raw sugar and molasses were shipped via charter ships to the East and Gulf Coast and then trucked to California. This certainly helped but didn't solve the problem. We couldn't ship out and we couldn't ship in so most small businesses were not receiving their needed inventory to operate. Some were closing, it was desperate times. We were somewhat fortunate because we had stocked up before the strike, however, our inventory was getting low, and it was necessary to ration. Some of our customers took it in stride and some didn't. Mr. Furusho, from Kauai Termite, gave Norm "hell" when we went to visit him. Many small businesses were forced to close, toilet paper was one of the commodities most affected. The island people had been through shipping strikes before. They knew that if you don't stock up on toilet paper in a situation like this, you just won't have any. Ti leaves work but not like toilet paper. So, hoarding takes place. All the stores were without toilet paper in short order. This even happens today. There might be a tsunami warning and people run out and buy toilet paper. Why toilet paper? It is cheap, light, and bulky. It would be very expensive to air freight.

Guess whose furniture and household items and motorcycles didn't get shipped? Bruce and Kip's. I initially leased a furnished condo so in that respect we were in good shape. Our motorcycles, our clothes, our tennis rackets and so much more were waiting at the docks in California. We were fortunate because the shipping strike was temporarily stopped when President Nixon invoked the Taft Hartley Act on October 4, 1971, about one month after I arrived in Hawaii. The Act allowed for an eighty-day cooling-off period. These eighty days were intended for the labor union (ILWU) and their employers Pacific Maritime Association (PMA), to work out their differences and resolve their disputes. It also allowed shipping to resume along the West Coast, Alaska, and Hawaii. Kip and I could get our items. However, there was a big delay due to all the backlog, but it finally arrived along with tons and tons of toilet paper and everything else you could imagine.

The people and businesses of Hawaii stocked up because this strike may not be over. It wasn't. The strike resumed after the eighty-day cooling-off period and this time with more anger and frustration than before. The strike resumed on January 17, 1972, and finally ended on February 7, 1972. The strike lasted a total of 130 days and shut all fifty-six West Coast ports. It was the longest ILWU strike in history. It was a tough time for many people and businesses, but we fared pretty well. We built up our inventory during the cooling-off period and we were able to air freight our fumigant, Vikane, Vikane SO^2F^2, at Dow Chemical's expense. Vikane came in 125-pound pressurized cylinders, from California to Hawaii. Air freighting Vikane would never be permitted today because of EPA standards.

When Kip arrived in Hawaii, he didn't have a job. I was able to line him up with an interview with Dow Chemical where he got a job working in their warehouse. It wasn't a great job, but it was a job. Kip is a hard worker and a bright guy. He and I had a lot of fun exploring Hawaii with our motorcycles out on the weekends and explore. During the time he was there, we probably went around the island of Oahu at least three times. My favorite trip is when we went up to Haleiwa to watch the surfers ride gigantic waves, some over forty feet high. Of course, we didn't go there to look at the girls in their bikinis. Then we went on through Waialua to Dillingham Airfield and watched gliders and then onto Kaena Point to watch the humpback whales spouting.

In California, we would go to the beaches during the summer a lot. The color of the water in Hawaii is a much deeper blue, the white caps are whiter, the sky is bluer, and the clouds are puffier and whiter. I was overwhelmed by Hawaii's beauty. Once you get to Kaena Point the road ends, except it is open for hikers and fishermen. At Kaena Point, there are several endangered animals including a variety of birds and the Hawaiian monk seal. Many of the plants are native to the area and do not exist anywhere else. To see Kaena Point from the south, you would have to go up the Waianae coastline and pass Nanakuli, Waianae, and Makaha. We did that the next weekend.

My job in Hawaii was such a great experience. I thoroughly enjoyed it and loved the people of Hawaii and the Hawaiian lifestyle. In addition, its beauty and variety amazed me. On one trip to the Big Island, I met up with Craig Wolters. Craig worked with his dad, Claire Wolters who at that time worked for Alii Termite and Pest Control. Craig was about my age and he and his dad had flown from Oahu to the Big Island in a leased two-passenger Cessna airplane. They both had their pilot's licenses and were skilled pilots. Craig offered to take me on a sightseeing flight. We probably flew for over an hour taking in the Big Island's diversity and beauty. I was awestruck as we flew over the Kilauea Volcano, which was erupting. Then Craig suggested that we come back and fly over it at night. We did, and what a treat we got. At night the lava flows are dynamic in their bright orange glow weaving down the sides of Kilauea. It was the most spectacular sight I have ever seen. I took plenty of pictures and had slides made. With my slide projector, I could view these photos at my leisure. My grandkids are wondering, what is a slide projector? I should say, google it, but I will explain.

A slide projector is a device that enlarges your slides. Well, now you may ask, what is a slide? A slide is a piece of film bordered by thin cardboard. The slides are then placed in a carousel, which holds about eighty slides which you can project onto a screen or blank wall and have a slideshow. Now you know how the term slideshow appears on your iPhone. My pictures came out great and my slideshow was a success. I think my carousel is in the attic and the slide projector is broken. I wish I could have taken those pictures on my iPhone and saved them to the cloud. We had beautiful clouds back fifty years ago, but we couldn't save anything in them.

On the weekends, if Kip and I weren't riding our motorcycles, we were playing tennis at Ala Moana Park as we were fairly evenly matched, we had some great times. We also went to the movies or the theater. Kip was a real theater buff. In high school and at Cal Poly he was in several productions, and he was good.

Ted Kimura, one of my customers and the owner of Island Termite, invited the two of us to a party with him and his friend Helen Ariyoshi. The host and hostess of the party were Harold and Mary Otani. This was our first party in Hawaii. It was a lot different than our frat parties that Kip and I were familiar with. The age range was probably 2–78. They would bring their whole family. There were probably twenty people, and the food was always fantastic. The food was mostly Asian and there was such a variety. Most of the guests brought something and Ted always brought deserts, he liked to eat it too, he was a big fellow. We enjoyed the Otani's and Ted and Helen. Helen was a very pretty Japanese lady. Her brother was our governor, George Ariyoshi. We met him on a few occasions at the Otani's parties.

Kip and I had a lot of fun everywhere we went, but I could tell he was having second thoughts about staying. For some reason, we weren't meeting girls and that was frustrating. He had about a year left to get his degree and he wasn't getting anywhere with his warehouse job. He decided to return to California to get his degree. I was going to lose my tennis buddy, my motorcycle companion, and my best friend. It was tough because Kip was an idea person and always looking for fun things to do. I was going to miss him. We had to arrange to ship his belongings back to California and make arrangements for me to move. When Kip left, I moved to a house in Kaaawa, (try to say that correctly) It is just past the Crouching Lion Inn and Restaurant. This house was shared with five people, and I can't remember how I heard about it. I know my rent was fairly cheap because I was very frugal. It took almost an hour to get there from my office on Kamakee Street in Honolulu. I had to drive through the Pali Tunnel on Likelike Hwy. and head north on Kahekili Hwy, which turns into Kamehameha Hwy. Ave. I had lived in Hawaii for about six months, and I was getting better at street names.

I was enjoying my job and I was relieved that the hot summer was over. For the most part, winters are very pleasant in Hawaii. A typical winter day is in the high 70s to the low 80s, sunny with passing showers and trade winds. The clouds are usually white and puffy. On rare occasions, you could get bad weather. If you live in Hawaii long enough you may witness a hurricane. Generally, hurricanes can form in the summer to fall months when the water is warmer. Hurricanes are infrequent and major hurricanes are even more infrequent. Since I was so new to Hawaii, I hadn't experienced a hurricane or a tsunami. As a kid, I had heard about Hurricane Dot hitting Hawaii. It was 1959 and I was eleven years old. Dot's effects were felt on all the islands and two indirect deaths resulted in Lanai. Dot made landfall on the island of Kauai. Winds of 103 mph and flooding caused major damage to telecommunications and sugarcane. Damage from Dot amounted to $6,000,000.

In Hawaii, we now get news of tropical storms or hurricanes approaching way in advance due to the new technologies in weather forecasting and GPS. Sometimes three, four, or five days in advance. We rarely know until the last minute if the hurricane will make landfall. Usually by that time all the toilet paper has disappeared from the stores. Another event in Hawaii that causes a TP shortage is a tsunami, or I should say tsunami warning. There was a major tsunami in Hawaii on April 1, 1946. This tsunami originated in the Aleutian Islands from an 8.6 magnitude earthquake. It traveled across the ocean at an estimated speed of 500 mph. The 55-foot wave hit Hilo town and did major destruction—173 people were killed and 163 were injured. As the wave receded many victims were swept out to sea. In Hilo, 488 buildings were demolished and 936 more were damaged. Maui lost seventy-seven homes and many other buildings on this April Fool's Day. Hawaii was caught off guard because of improper warnings. In 1949 the Pacific Tsunami Warning Center came about to provide a reliable warning system regarding tsunamis. . There have been 100 tsunamis recorded in Hawaii since records were first kept about 200 years ago. Most have caused little or no damage. Now we get warnings and the TP is quickly gone.

I managed to live a few more months in Kaaawa. I had my sights on buying a home. The most reasonably priced homes were on the other side of the island. I had my eyes on a development above Ewa Beach on the gentle slopes of the mountains. New homes were starting at around $35,000. That could get you a three-bedroom, two-bathroom house with a two-car carport and about 7,000 square feet of land. Housing in Hawaii is expensive compared to other parts of the United States. I had $3,000 in savings but needed $5,000 for the down payment. I was impatient as normal so I talked to my mom, and I was nervous. I asked her if I could borrow $2,000. I had never asked to borrow money before. With my jobs during high school, I was self-sufficient as I paid for my college and housing. I didn't need a lot. But now, I wanted a house. I was so happy when my mother said they would loan me the money.

We worked out a financial agreement and for two years I would pay it back with principal and interest at the prevailing rate, which was around 8%. I bought a four-bedroom, two-bath home with an unobstructed view of the ocean. It had a larger lot, close to 10,000 square feet. The house was built on post and piers and was single-wall construction. It was a rectangle and it looked like all the other houses in the neighborhood. I couldn't have been prouder. The price was $39,000. There were no houses for about five miles on the makai (ocean) side, below me, just green sugarcane fields and the ocean. On the mauka (mountain) side there were probably 400 homes above me. I just hoped they were built well and that I wasn't in a landslide zone because I was a little concerned about the post and pier construction. The posts were 4" X 4"s, sitting on a concrete pier, which was about one square foot at the base and about one foot high. The posts on the makai side of the house were about twelve feet high as my land sloped significantly. These piers sat on lava or a very thin layer of soil. What happens if it floods? What happens if we get 100 mph winds? Single wall construction? I had questions but did my research before buying. These houses are strong.

When I lived in Kaaawa, which is on the windward side of the island, we had beautiful sunrises and significant rainfall. Makakilo is on the leeward side of the island. It gets much less rain and has beautiful sunsets. My living room looked onto my deck, which looked onto the green sugarcane fields, which looked over the ocean, at the most beautiful sunsets in the world. I have many beautiful pictures from my deck of fantastic sunsets, which are in a slide carousel in my attic without a projector and not in the cloud.

Now I am the proud owner of a four-bedroom house with no wife or kids. It would be mighty lonely if I were to stay there by myself. The first year, to the best of my recollection, I had John Cappadonna stay for the summer. John was a freshman at Cal Poly and was in our fraternity when I was a senior. John still lives on Maui, and I see him periodically. Dave Takacs was also a fraternity brother and lived at this house for about three years. He eventually bought a townhouse in Makakilo. He moved away from Maui, got married, and is living in the Bay area. Also, Ed Manko, a captain in the Air Force, from Hickam Air Force Base, stayed at the house for a couple of years. They all paid their fair rent, which was a big help to me.

I was a homebody and I still am. I loved working on house projects and landscaping. Landscaping the Makakilo house was challenging because the lot had a steep slope with very little top soil. I built a rock wall on the back boundary and brought in topsoil and planted a lawn, and it was the prettiest lawn in the neighborhood. The lawn had a significant slope at the front and the neighbor kids would bring cardboard and slide on it. I was able to pay my mortgage and my loan to my parents with the help of my roommates. Mom had mellowed, in our letters, we would discuss politics, world matters, family, and so forth. Letter writing brought us much closer. I also realized that our viewpoints were very similar and even our characteristics were similar. We would both get upset rather quickly; we would cool down quickly and hold little if any grudges. She was honest, fair, tough, and mellowed as she aged, as I have done. I corresponded with Mom almost weekly while living in Hawaii. Mom was an intelligent person, well-read, and a very good writer. I looked forward to her letters. I realized that we had so much in common. I went through a lot of frustration growing up with her because she did not have a lot of patience with me and I was sensitive. Although I now lived in Hawaii and my parents lived in California, I got much closer with my mother, in fact she was a wonderful Mom but just a little short on patience.

CHAPTER 12

Meeting Evelyn January 1, 1974, to July 6, 1974

On December 31, 1973, my roommates, Ed, Dave, and myself, went to a New Year's Eve party with Ed's Air Force friends. We met three girls who were together. I danced with one of them a few times and in our conversation, I asked if she and her two friends would like to join us at another party. The Otani's, Mary, and Harold Otani always had the best New Year's Eve party, there would be great food, conversation, and fireworks. She talked to her friends and said they would like to join us. I was surprised. They followed as we went to the Otani's. As the evening went on, I started talking to Evelyn, one of the other girls and she would listen, but she hardly said a word.

She was so quiet and so cute. The fact that she listened was good enough for me. We had fun and I found out that she was on vacation and was going to return to San Francisco in a few days. After we brought in the New Year with thousands of firecrackers, we went our separate ways, although she was in my heart. The next evening, I called her and asked her to join me for dinner with Steve Cooley and his new bride Roseanne. Steve and Roseanne were honeymooning in Honolulu from California. I hadn't seen Steve for a long time and was anxious to catch up on old times and meet his bride. Evelyn accepted my invitation. I got the necessary information on where to pick her up, I was feeling very good because I met a good person. I watched a football game or two during the day and went to pick her up at her parent's home in Kalihi.

When I arrived, she came out quickly to avoid introducing me. However, I was greeted at the door by these cute boys, one probably three and the other around six. When the door closed, they ran to the window to watch us leave. I will never lose that memory because it was so cute. Evelyn and I joined Steve and

Roseanne and had a great time and a great dinner. I felt very comfortable with Evelyn although she didn't say much, she was listening. Evelyn was leaving shortly. We agreed to write letters. which are in the attic with the slides. Now I was getting letters from both Evelyn and Mom. I enjoyed getting them and I enjoyed sending them. Although, I was now spending over my budget on postage. I was very tight. In 1971 when I moved from southern California to Hawaii, Evelyn moved from Hawaii to southern California. Evelyn first lived in Torrance, in an apartment with another girl from Hawaii with whom she had previously worked. Evelyn never thought she was going to leave her parent's house. She was twenty-five years old and felt she would be there for the rest of her life. Evelyn's father was very strict, and he wanted her to care for him and her mother. Evelyn made a very bold decision when she told her parents that she was moving to California. This shy and somewhat insecure girl was ready for a change. This change is just what she needed, away from home, she gained confidence.

Evelyn, born in the Philippines, started her life in Dingras, Ilocos Norte, Philippines, on May 9, 1946. Her mother, Alejandra was 8½ months pregnant with Evelyn and journeyed, from Baguio to Dingras, the hometown of her father, Gregorio. Evelyn's aunties were to receive Alejandra to prepare her for Evelyn's birth. Their house was a bamboo, one-room, house with no running water or electricity. Evelyn was healthy and ready to join the world. She was delivered in the same manner as her older brothers and sisters. Within a month Alejandra was able to bring Evelyn back to Baguio to be with her family. Baguio is a beautiful city and is known as the summer capital of the Philippines with its nice cool climate, sitting almost a mile above sea level. The city was surrounded by pine trees, mossy plants, and orchids to mention a few. However, over the past few decades, many of the pines have been cut and human modification has taken place. Baguio has lost some of its charm with development.

As a young child, Evelyn remembers rolling and smoking tobacco and sliding down the mountainside in cardboard boxes. She had her hanabata days too. The schools were taught in English because of the influence of the US after the Spanish American War. Evelyn spoke the Ilocano dialect at home with her family which is the third largest language in the Philippines after Tagalog and English. She lived in a very modest home, as they were quite poor. Gregorio was a policeman eking out a meager income. Evelyn has three brothers and three sisters and one passed at an early age. Evelyn's oldest brother is Teddy, then Franklin, Loida, Ester, Evelyn, and Greg. Her father came to Hawaii to try to make a better life. It was in 1946, that Alejandra was pregnant with Evelyn when he made the long journey over the Pacific Ocean to Hawaii. Many Ilocanos made this trek in hopes of a better life. because the sugar and pineapple plantations were recruiting workers.

Gregorio was a hard worker and was very careful with his money. He sacrificed and saved and sent money home to his family. He wanted to save enough money to go back to Baguio. While Gregorio was in Hawaii, Alejandra was raising the family. They were both very dedicated parents, sacrificing for a better life. Teddy joined his dad in Hawaii when he was seventeen and Franklin came a year later. When Evelyn was around five years old, Gregorio returned to Baguio for a short time. It was the first time Evelyn saw her father, also it was long enough to leave Alejandra pregnant with her sixth child, Baby Greg was born approximately nine months after his father's departure. When Evelyn was eleven years old, the plans had changed from Gregorio wanting to return to Baguio to wanting his family to move to Hawaii. Alejandra, Loida, Ester, Evelyn, and Greg boarded a passenger ship in Manila and fourteen days later, after many stops, entered Pearl Harbor. This was not a luxury cruise ship.

Hawaii was beautiful but where they were going to live was not. Evelyn calls it the slums off King Street in Honolulu. Because of Gregorio's and Alejandra's thriftiness, they were able to buy a modest house on Liliha Street approximately a year later. They continued to save their money and later bought the Kalihi house where I picked up Evelyn for our date, which was a nice two-story house.

It must have been February when I got to see Evelyn again. NAMCO scheduled a sales meeting in the bay area. Perfect, I can see Evelyn. I wrote to her to tell her about the meeting, and she was excited as I was. We arranged to see each other. John Herr, my "Big Brother" in my fraternity, and his wife Suzanne lived in Santa Rosa. Evelyn and I drove from San Francisco to their home and spent the night with them. We had a great time. Evelyn didn't say much but she listened well. They liked her. My trip was short, back in Hawaii, we resumed our letter writing. Calls from Hawaii to San Francisco were expensive so I only called her on special occasions. Through our letter writing, I was getting to know Evelyn. I liked whom I was getting to know. I was falling in love. Our letters were getting romantic.

In March, I was on a sales trip to Kauai. It is such a beautiful island and I was thinking of Evelyn. I was thinking about proposing. I called her the first night there and she was very surprised that I called because she knew it was out of my budget. I chickened out. Still on Kauai for another day, I couldn't get her off my mind. I called again and didn't chicken out. I proposed. She said, "Are you sure?" I said yes. That was the best decision I have ever made. To proceed, it would be proper for me to meet her parents and family and for her to meet mine. Evelyn arranged to fly to Los Angeles to meet my family and I went to meet Evelyn's family. Evelyn was picked up at the airport by my parents and Bonnie, my twin. Evelyn stayed with my parents for two days. On the second day, they went to my sister Julie's house for a family dinner.

Julie is a tremendous cook. I know without a doubt, that Evelyn would have loved to cook also. Pat, Pam, Bonnie, Julie, and Mom and Dad was there to approve my choice. Also, my brother-in-law and some of my nieces and nephews were there. They all approved. I knew they would. Because I wrote to Mom all the time, she knew Evelyn through my correspondence. Evelyn and I were the first in our family to have an interracial marriage. My brother-in-law John, Julie's husband, is a very conservative Irishman. He highly approved of my choice. I knew I had a winner. Evelyn wrote to me about her experience with my family. She also was impressed with them. It may have been the same weekend that I met her family at Teddy's house. Teddy, Evelyn's oldest brother and his wife Lynn, plus Franklin and Jean and Ester and Alfred and her parents, Alejandra and Gregorio, and Evelyn's nieces and nephews were there to meet Evelyn's future husband. It was a very harmonious evening. I enjoyed her family and they seemed to enjoy me. I got to meet those two little boys who saw Evelyn and me off on our first date. The oldest was Freddy and the youngest was Van. These two boys were sons of Ester and Alfred.

We continued to write a few more letters as she was planning her move back to Honolulu before giving her two weeks' notice. We set July 6, 1974, for the big day. Evelyn was soon back and now we were able to get to know each other. I quickly found out that she was particular, very particular. In addition, she is a very good planner and a great cook. I was so used to doing everything myself, from cooking liver, house cleaning to yard work to being the handyman. My cooking was terrible. I often bought liver because it was cheap and easy to cook. I would make liver sandwiches. She soon took over and my life was going to change. Although the wedding was still a few months away, Evelyn lived at her Kalihi home, and I lived in Makakilo. In the '70s many looked down upon couples living together before marriage.

I would often go to see Evelyn at her parent's house. Her mother, Alejandra, was a small quiet lady, who loved to cook for me. Mommy, as I was told to address her, was a great cook. It was mostly Filipino food and so tasty we grew very close. Before I met Mommy, Evelyn told her that I owned a house in Makakilo. Not many people my age owned homes. Mommy's reply to Evelyn was "He must be divorced." Both she and Daddy were skeptical of a haole marrying their youngest daughter. Daddy made a statement before Evelyn moved to California, "All you want to do is find one haole and he is going to leave you." He said it with more colorful words and in Ilocano. I had to convince her parents that I was worthy of her hand in marriage. Whatever I did, worked. I loved and respected them, and they were growing to trust me. Daddy was a man of few words to me, primarily because Ilocano was his first language. We loved eating together and watching boxing. I could see how Evelyn became so neat. Mommy kept a very tidy house and Daddy kept a very nice yard and an immaculate car. He would shine it every day.

CHAPTER 13

Getting Married July 6, 1974

As Evelyn and I got to know each other better, we realized we needed to learn to compromise. Even though Evelyn was very quiet, she still had a mind of her own. Before our engagement, we were both very independent and in those "getting to know each other" months, we had some disagreements, but we were able to resolve them. I think we were both convinced that we made the right choice, and neither of us wanted to back out now. The wedding was planned, and the invitations were sent. My twin Bonnie and sister Pam were coming to the wedding but my parents decided not to attend the wedding because they had just visited me at the beginning of the year in Hawaii, and they met and highly approved of Evelyn. They thought it wasn't necessary, however, I wanted them to be there and even offered to pay their way. That just made Mom mad. Oh well, my mom is stubborn, and I understood.

We had a beautiful outdoor wedding on the grounds of the Kahala Hilton. Evelyn looked gorgeous in her white flowing wedding dress, and I looked pretty dapper in my tuxedo. We shared our wedding vows in front of a cascading waterfall with my little nephew Van, who saw us off on our first date, was the ring bearer, and my niece Sherry who was our flower girl. It was beautiful. Our wedding reception was held at a banquet hall at the Ala Moana Center. It was very festive, and the food was ono, at the reception Evelyn did a solo hula for me, which was unexpected and beautiful. We spent our honeymoon at the Kahala Hilton. Evelyn planned a beautiful wedding, reception, and honeymoon, now it was my turn to plan our honeymoon vacation. I selected the Big Island where we stayed on the slopes between Mauna Loa and Mauna Kea for a vacation that we would never forget. Our accommodations were very rustic, we were well protected, and the price was very affordable. It was a little barren as we stayed at the State of Hawaii cabins off Saddle Road next to Pohakuloa Military Training Area. The bunk beds weren't very comfortable or romantic, so we put the mattresses on the floor. I liked it, Evelyn didn't. It was reasonable and it was also remote, so we didn't have to eat out and it was peaceful, hardly anyone was there.

After our honeymoon vacation, life had to get back to normal. Evelyn already had a job. When she moved from San Francisco to Hawaii, she got a direct transfer from her federal job. It wasn't long after our wedding that my boss Norm asked me if I would be willing to move to Houston and open a Texas branch for NAMCO. I discussed it with Evelyn, and we were both interested. Pam Zinn, Norm's assistant, was going to be my inside salesperson.

Pam was a real dynamo. About one month before going to Houston, Pam gave her two weeks' notice saying she had a change of heart. The gal hired to replace Pam was now mine. Lucky me. Evelyn and I moved at the beginning of 1975, and we bought a nice brick home in a manicured neighborhood. NAMCO agreed to buy our Makakilo house for around $58,000 which was the average of three appraisals. They advanced me the proceeds minus the mortgage and estimated closing costs and we went on a house-buying trip to Texas to start a new chapter in our lives.

CHAPTER 14

Transfer to Houston; Jennifer 1975–1976

We were going to miss our Makakilo view and so many things about Hawaii, including Evelyn's family, my customers, friends, and coworkers. Houston was going to be a new challenge and I love a new challenge and Evelyn wanted to do it. After getting established in our new home, I was ready for this new challenge. Norm came to help me open the Houston office to call on key accounts. Shortly after we opened, our office salesperson quit because of me and I was glad because we were able to fill the void quickly and with a much more compatible employee. It wasn't much later NAMCO was bought by Allied Equities, a holding company that Norm hated. Allied Equities drained the old NAMCO. It was no fun trying to open a new branch with very little inventory. On November 30, 1974, Allied Equities dissolved, leaving NAMCO in a mess. We were taken over by Van Waters and Rogers, a chemical supplier based out of Seattle, which eventually became Univar. All this was happening in my first year in Texas. In addition to all the confusion, I did not like my new boss. I loved Norm and highly respected him. My new boss was based out of Dallas wasn't very bright, and he wasn't honest. I don't deal well with dishonesty. I liked my customers, and I liked my job and I tried to make things work.

Once we got inventory in good shape, I was on the road quite a bit. I got three speeding tickets in one year because I was driving all the time in wide-open country. I called on pest control operators in Houston, Galveston, San Antonio, Austin, Corpus Christi, and I think I went to Brownsville one time, enjoying calling on new accounts in new areas. Evelyn and I made good friends in San Antonio and Austin and we loved being tourists and seeing new places.

My grandmother, Aunt Dot, came to visit Evelyn and me. She stayed about a week and during that time we went to Lake Charles, Louisiana to visit my Aunt Mary, Dad's youngest stepsister. Driving into Louisiana, Evelyn and I got strange "whites only" stares as if "you two don't belong here" stares. Her being Filipino and me being Caucasian must have triggered those stares. We both felt it and we weren't used to it. I told Evelyn not to use the bathrooms that say whites only. We had a nice visit with Aunt Mary, but I did not like Lake Charles, Aunt Dot was a super grandmother, and we enjoyed her visit.

We had fun in Texas and our ping-pong games certainly improved while there. Most houses have formal and informal living rooms. We didn't need a formal living room, we're from Hawaii, so we converted it to our ping-pong room where we played almost every night. The Houston weather was quite different from Honolulu. The crack of thunder was so loud and the lightning so close, the winters colder but relatively mild, and the summers hot, hot, and muggy, much more so than in Hawaii.

Evelyn was pregnant with Jennifer, our first daughter. Jen was born on "Leap Year Day" 1976, our Texas baby. Evelyn was a natural mother, and I was an unnatural father. I had never been around babies, never changed a diaper, and I was never woken up all hours of the night by crying. I learned a little through Evelyn's patience. Mommy came for nearly two months and that was a big help.

I had a strange medical experience happen to me while in Houston. I was having some memory loss, known medically as amnesia. We went to dinner one night with a couple who lived directly behind us. They were young doctors, Dr. and Dr. Darcey. The next day I couldn't remember going out with them, what we did, or what we ate. I couldn't remember anything. Evelyn mentioned to the Darcey's of my strange memory loss. They suggested that I see a neurologist and provided a name of a very reputable neurologist. We made the appointment, and I was told by the doctor that I needed to be under observation while sleeping and awake. In a short time, I was admitted to the hospital where I stayed for nearly a week. My tests were not conclusive. My doctor prescribed a low dosage of Dilantin, an antiseizure medication. I later found out that this wasn't the first time I had memory loss. Before marrying Evelyn, I was an usher in Gordy Wilson's wedding while I was living in California. I was probably twenty-two or twenty-three. I was shown a picture of myself at the wedding party as an usher but I have no recollection of that whatsoever. Gordy was a great friend of mine. I should have remembered.

There may have been many more occasions of amnesia, but I can't remember. I was diagnosed as possibly having Transient Epileptic Amnesia. (TEA) This condition is very rare. According to literature, memory loss is due to underlying temporal lobe epilepsy. TEA is a form of focal seizure of adult-onset epilepsy. Focal seizures are located on one side of the brain and signs of a person having a focal seizure are minimal. The person may have an aura; a strange sense of smell or taste, twitching, or a feeling of déjà vu. It is not to be confused with a grand mal seizure, now called tonic-clonic seizure, tonic meaning stiffening and clonic meaning rhythmical jerking. This seizure affects both lobes of the brain, if one has a tonic-clonic seizure, the person will become unconscious, and violent muscle contractions will occur.

Stress and confusion were getting to me and I was fed up with my boss. I decided I had enough. We liked Houston, but we missed family and we missed Hawaii. I didn't want to go back to Oahu, it was too crowded and not the most pleasant location to raise a young family. I was focused on the outer islands. I had never quit a job before other than the carwash. I decided I had enough and it was time for a change.

CHAPTER 15

Move to Maui and Early Days of Maui Fumigation 1976–1980

One of my pest control customers from the Big Island, Glen Morphis, told me before I left Hawaii, "If you ever want to come back to Hawaii, give me a call, we can probably do something together." Evelyn and I wanted to go to the Big Island; we loved Hilo. I called Glen letting him know that I was considering his earlier suggestion. He told me that he was starting a fumigation company on Maui and asked if I would be willing to invest and be a 50% owner. I had to get Evelyn's approval, but I felt good about it. I trusted Glen. I would put in $7,000 and manage the pest control operations, draw a small salary, and own half of Maui Fumigation. Evelyn was willing to take this bold move. We had to sell our Houston house and move our items to Maui, that was an ordeal. I rented a big U-Haul truck, loaded our household belongings, and drove from Houston to Los Angeles.

Evelyn and Jennifer went on to Honolulu and waited for me. My sister Bonnie helped me at the docks to unload the U-Haul at the container yard. I was soon on my way to Maui where houses were nearly triple the cost of houses in Houston. I had to learn a new job, knowing the technical aspects of fumigation, but I had never fumigated a house. I wasn't afraid of challenges; however, I probably should have been. Fumigation is hard, physical work, but I have never been afraid of hard work. I had some regrets at first, going from a sales job to an outright laborer, but I loved working outdoors and I was working on Maui. What can I say? About a year after starting with Glen, I offered to buy him out. We came to terms. I was to pay him $20,000, $1,000 per month for twenty months and I also signed a non-compete agreement for five years. With the non-compete, we could not provide pest control or termite treatments other than fumigation. That was very hard; we struggled, but we did it. I was the lead fumigator for five years, from 1976 to 1981.

Not too long after we arrived on Maui, I sought out a neurologist to follow up as requested by my Houston doctor. At that time, I was on mild antiseizure medication because of my memory loss. The doctor on Maui recommended that I take five times the amount of medication that I was prescribed in Houston. I rebelled; the Houston doctors were so thorough and I thought my Maui doctor was a quack. Actually, in 1978 Maui didn't even have a full-time neurologist. The neurologist I saw on Maui was based in Oahu and would come to Maui a few days out of the month. After I saw him, I stopped my medication abruptly and in a short time, I had a grand mal seizure. Stopping antiseizure medications abruptly is not good, and unfortunately, I found out. An ambulance had to take me to the hospital. I think I was in better shape than Evelyn; she was a nervous wreck. Witnessing my seizure was a horrible experience for her. The blood coming from my mouth and my comatose state and convulsing scared the bejabbers out of her. After my first grand mal seizure, I was having occasional focal seizures, and within a year, I had another grand mal seizure. This time I was fumigating and fortunately, I had just gotten off the roof of a house. If I had this seizure a few minutes earlier, I may not have been here to tell you about it. I saw another neurologist, Dr. Darenfeldt, who had all the right credentials. He did up my medication a little and I went along with him.

Our second daughter, Jill was born on April 10, 1978. I would come home from work as a dirty dad and husband because as a fumigator you can't get the dirt out of your hands. You could wash and wash but some of the dirt would always remain because it was under your skin. When we fumigate, we seam tarps by rolling them together and then using metal pins, like heavy-duty metal clothespins, to keep the tarps from separating. When rolling the seams your hands are in constant contact with the dirty tarps. You would create calluses on calluses, rubbing the dirt deeper into your skin. The most enjoyable time was when rolling seams on a flat hot roof The intense heat from the tarps would burn the calluses off, and you would start the cycle again with very tender skin, burning with every roll and adding new dirt and grit embedded in your fingers. Then new calluses would form over the dirt.

There were advantages to fumigation work. You didn't have to go to the gym, I was in excellent shape and I could climb ladders with 140 pounds of tarp on my shoulders. I weighed about 150 pounds. Sometimes I climbed one, two, and three stories high. As the roof man, you get over the fear of heights because you are always on the top and at the edges of roofs. There was one house that we fumigated in Kipahulu, Sam Pryor's house, that overlooked the Kipahulu gulch. It was a beautiful house, with a gazebo attached. The gazebo was at the edge of the gulch and the gulch was probably at least 200 feet deep and a sheer drop. When I got on the roof with the tarp I was petrified. As I looked down, my heart raced as I lay prone on the roof moving the tarp slowly with one hand until the top was covered. We got it done as my legs were shaking upon my return to the ground.

In the '70s we weren't required to have fall protection as we are today. Initially, we did a lot of work in Hana. Mr. Dempsey Villiarimo was in charge of maintenance at Hotel Hana Maui. We got together and discussed the prospects of doing business in Hana, a small remote community, where Dempsey knew practically everyone. We paid Dempsey a finders-fee and I would go estimate the houses. We got almost every job. The drive to Hana is fifty-two miles from Wailuku. The road at that time was terrible, mostly paved but full of potholes. It was windy and sometimes treacherous. The good thing in those days was that very few drove on the road because it was so bad. It would take nearly three hours to get to Hana from Wailuku. Recently the road has been improved significantly and it takes longer to get to Hana. With our increase of population and tourism Hana Hwy. has traffic congestion.

On one trip we had more work than we could handle. Dempsey said his nephew, Barry could help. Barry started to work, and he did pretty well. I brought him on full time as he was willing to move to Wailuku. He asked if I could hire his cousin, Melvin Moiha. I did and the three of us did a lot of fumigation together. Melvin had a speech impediment, but he didn't let that get to him because he was so funny and fun to work with. Barry, on the other hand, was a grouch at times. When working with a crew eight hours a day, it is important to get along. Overall, we got along well.

We squeaked by with Evelyn, mothering our two daughters as a stay-at-home mom, and me working hard to support the family and in Hana, about 1/3 of the time. It wasn't too long after arriving on Maui that we purchased a lot in a new subdivision in Waiehu Heights. We had the corner lot with the most spectacular ocean and mountain view. Not quite as nice as Makakilo, where we had beautiful sunsets but now, we have beautiful sunrises. Our house was designed by Uwe Schultz who was a young architect at the time and willing to design an affordable house for us. He was a young architect at the time and willing to design an affordable home for us. After it was built, I built a rock retaining wall and landscaped it. With a wrap-around deck, it was very attractive. Waiehu Heights was a subdivision with a lot of young couples and kids and it was a great start for our family on Maui.

When the business was just starting, the phone didn't ring very often so we had an answering service so we didn't need an office. We did rent some yard space in Wailuku to park our truck and warehouse our supplies. Our warehouse consisted of a Sears utility building, approximately 6'X 6'. As the business grew, the phone started ringing and Evelyn agreed to work with me, and we rented a small warehouse. It had a small office, a little space for our tarps, and equipment, and room to park our fumigation truck, with little room to spare. Evelyn would prepare for the day and bring the playpen so the kids were content. That was the start of our family business. In 1978 I lost my two Hana boys. After they left, I remember having to fumigate one house by myself.

It is difficult to find fumigators because it is hard work, but I wanted things to work out. As a backup, in the winter of 1978, I got a real estate license to supplement my meager income. I sold some real estate with Donna Ting, broker for Tri Isle Realty. One of my clients, Willie and Irene Chun became close friends of ours and their daughter Pam, worked with us at Maui Fumigation one summer. However, it was hard to do both fumigation and real estate. When I was fumigating, I was always dirty, which wasn't the best situation for real estate. I decided to leave real estate behind and fully concentrate on Maui Fumigation. It was about then when Albert Kuuana started working with me and he turned out to be excellent and was very quiet but smart. Shortly after Albert started working, his friend David joined us when we were in our summer months, and getting busy.

We landed our first condo project. We fumigated thirteen buildings at Kihei Kai Nani however, David didn't last long, but Albert had another friend in mind.

He suggested we hire his close friend, a young Filipino boy, Clem Torricer. I hired Clem and the three of us worked well together as a team. Clem and I are still working together, in fact, we have been working together for forty-two years, but who's counting? I love working with Clem and he does with me. We have learned so much together and from each other.

When Clem started, I now had two very quiet people whom I was working with. They weren't like Melvin. I don't know if it was because I was one Haole, but conversations were far and few between. There wasn't any joking around, although I missed that, our work was done proficiently.

The fumigation business is challenging. The challenge was to get the jobs, but the biggest challenge was to complete the job when it was windy. The central part of Maui is generally very windy, especially in the 1970s. I read an article recently about the change of wind patterns in Maui due to global warming, on average the wind has declined about 27% now compared to the 1970s–1990s. When we first started fumigation, the tarps weren't as durable as the ones used today. In high winds, the tarps can rip, and they are not cheap to replace and all our effort could be in vain. As the company grew, we started fumigating larger and larger buildings. To secure the tarps we would roll boards into the seams and clamp them along with the pinning. In Kihei, the winds were generally calm in the mornings and by three or four o'clock, would pick up and could become quite strong. On this particular day, we covered a 10-unit condominium building at Kihei Garden Estates. We finished around 4:00 p.m. The winds were around 15–20 mph which is just right.

In fumigation, it is nice to have some wind to cool you off however, when it's blowing 25–35 mph you can have problems. We stuck around for a little while and left feeling very confident. The stronger winds started about one hour after we left. I got a call from Pam Bello, the property manager, letting me know that our tarps were ripping. I called Clem and Albert and told them that we had a blowout, a fumigation term for tarps ripping or seams coming undone. I picked them up so we could try to save the fumigation. Pam and her husband Ed were there. By that time the wind was gusting well over 30 mph. and it was dark. There was no way we could save our hard work. Pam and Ed were so great and understanding. I stood there helplessly, and Pam hugged me. Pam and Ed became close friends and chose us for every job and have become one of our most reliable customers. They knew we gave it our all. It wasn't much later that rip-stop tarps became available which are much stronger and just a little heavier.

Clem and Albert were both smart, and as I mentioned, quiet. We would ride together in the cab of the fumigation truck, and I was the only one talking. The radio reception was terrible when going to Hana. In Hana, we would often stay at the Waianapanapa Cabins like the one I took Evelyn to on our honeymoon, but we didn't sleep on the floor. In Hana, we fumigated Hotel Hana Maui, most of the homes, and almost every church. We fumigated one church mistaking it for another. We told the pastor we were sorry for our mistake and he said we will pay you, it needed fumigation. That represents the spirit of the Hana people. One time after a day of fumigating at the hotel we showered and were ready to relax, Albert asked if it was okay if he smoked a joint. I said okay, as long as I can try. I smoked my first weed with Clem and Albert and I hated it. I felt paranoid. I tried one other time later with Kip while visiting the mainland. Same feeling. Weed wasn't for me; I'll stick with my beer.

I am an idea person, some good and some bad. Since the business was starting to grow, I got this brilliant idea. Our company should buy a condo in Kihei so we could provide a place for our customers to stay while their home is fumigated during the overnight process. Fumigation customers must stay out of their home for one night for their house to be fumigated. Scheduling was a pain in the ass. I got sisters, Patty and Pam to invest with me but this investment didn't live up to my expectations. It was such a hassle to schedule it for the business. The vacation rental market was soft, and we sold in this soft market and all lost money. Overall, things were starting to pick up for Maui Fumigation. With Clem and Albert on board and Evelyn in the office, we were starting to see a light at the end of the tunnel.

CHAPTER 16

Jill, Jeff, and Jennifer Growing up With the Business 1978–1980

Back home Jennifer and Jill were growing up fast and Evelyn was now pregnant with Jeff. born on October 14, 1979. Our business was picking up a little, but we were still struggling. With three kids and a struggling business, we had to work that much harder because at times I had to forgo a paycheck and Evelyn wasn't getting paid. We had approximately one more year of our non-compete. It was hard to do strictly fumigation without pest control and termite services, we were scratching the bottom of the barrel. At certain points, I was almost ready to throw in the towel but Albert and Clem stuck with me during the lean times. Evelyn was so supportive, and I became determined to stick it out.

The winters were generally slow, and the summers were fairly busy. As the summer approached, Maui Fumigation was starting to get busier. In Hawaii, to fumigate, the crew must be under the direct supervision of a licensed fumigator and I was the Maui Fumigation licensed fumigator. To get a fumigation license, the applicant had to have been on fifty fumigations and be able to pass the exam. Filling out the State of Hawaii application was the hardest part. Albert and Clem had plenty of fumigations but were reluctant to take the exam. I was stuck until I could get another licensed fumigator. I was starting to get a lot of Filipino customers as I would measure one house I would be referred to their neighbors and their neighbor would refer me to their neighbor and a friend and so on.

My five-year non-compete was almost over. In those five years, my main competition was Dick's Fumigation, a well-established, family-run business, Xtermco, an Oahu-based company, and Coverseal, a fumigation company run by

Chuck Harvey, a notorious drinker. The population of Maui was small in comparison to today, but it was growing very quickly. In 1976 when we arrived, Maui had a population of about 58,000. The population was growing rapidly as was tourism and construction and those areas needed pest control. The future was looking a little brighter and our business did grow. Albert and Clem were both excellent fumigators and finally took the fumigation license test, and both passed with ease. Our five-year non-compete was over and now we could do pest control, termite work, and fumigation. We had a small amount of money in the bank at this time and our fumigation tarps and equipment were in reasonable condition. People were starting to recognize our company mostly by word of mouth and with some meager advertising. We were at least out there now, not like the first few years, we had a good reputation, and our prices were in the middle range, not the cheapest and not the most expensive.

John Saling owned a one-man pest-control company and was referring his fumigation leads to us. He came to me one day and said he wanted to sell his business. We worked out a deal which was good for John, but it was great for Maui Fumigation. It got us some good pest control accounts and very good termite accounts. He had worked with several contractors and construction was picking up. We got in at the right time. With our non-compete, we couldn't do this work, but now we could. We moved Clem from fumigation to handle the work from this new acquisition. Quintin Molina came on as an experienced fumigator from Dicks. Evelyn was getting overwhelmed in the office, and she hired additional office help and I was freed up to do sales. I went to condo management companies, real estate offices, and building contractors to secure work and bids. From our meager beginning, Maui Fumigation grew to become the largest pest, termite, and fumigation company on Maui. Towards the end, we ran three, three-man fumigation crews in the summer. Albert ran one crew, Quintin another, and Norman Lani another. Norman had come to us from another company. We were the leaders in fumigation and quite busy in our termite department, but our pest control was our weak link.

CHAPTER 17

Running/Delmores and Kids 1979–1982

On July 4, 1979, I met a person who had a big influence on my life, Tom Delmore. Evelyn and I took the kids to the Intercontinental Hotel fireworks show in Kihei. Jeff was eight months old at the time, Jill two, and Jennifer was four years old. They sat in amazement as the sky was full of a dynamic firework display. Evelyn had seen Young Delmore, an attractive Korean lady at the display. They had met earlier in our neighborhood while Young was walking Brian in his stroller and Evelyn was walking Jeff in his stroller. They didn't know each other well but recognized one another. Young brought their blanket close to ours to sit and watch the display. I met Tom, Young's husband, Brian, who was the same age as Jeff, and Kimberly who was the same age as Jennifer. We all became instant friends. Young was born in North Korea in December of 1947 and fled to South Korea with her family near the start of the Korean War. It has been estimated that there were over two million North Koreans who fled to South Korea during this time.

Tom, is Caucasian like me, is nerdy-looking, and is nerdy. We both had mixed marriages which are very common in Hawaii. We got acquainted that evening and I found out that Tom was an avid runner. That evening he asked me if I would like to join him on a run. We lived about ten houses apart in Waiehu Heights so the next day I joined him on a run after work. We ran from my house to Waihee School, there we took a few sips of water and ran back to my house. It is approximately five miles. He was surprised that I could do this run at an eight-minute-per-mile pace. I was in good shape because I was fumigating. I got hooked on running from that day on. We started running five to six miles per day and got to know each other well through our running. He is smart, has a fantastic memory, an avid reader is five years older than me. He graduated from the University of Wisconsin, then worked with the IRS for about eighteen years when I met him.

As we ran, we would talk about everything, from diets to politics, to how much he hated his job at the IRS. Politically we both lean to the left, but he tends to lean harder than I do. As he ran with me, he coached me insisting I buy the right running gear and keep a log of our runs for times and the distances. Tom was an experienced runner at that time having a few marathons under his belt, including Honolulu. As we ran, our training runs became longer, and our times became faster. He suggested that we join the Valley Isle Road Runners (VIRR). This was the Maui running club and they organized many runs where we had great times and met some fantastic people. In addition to running, our families became the best of friends, Jeff and Brian played together and Jill and Jennifer played with Kimberly. On the weekends we would have them over for dinner or we would go to their house for dinner we would go to the beach together, go hiking or go to a (VIRR) event. We were pretty much inseparable.

In one of our early running conversations, Tom informed me that he had been a three-pack-a-day cigarette smoker and drank a six-pack of beer daily. When he came to Hawaii in 1974, he quit smoking cold turkey but he didn't give up the beer, but maybe slowed down just a bit. He got me into beer drinking and we would drink together. Tom was a little impulsive as with the cigarettes, he could radically change his diet. Before I met him, he weighed close to 200 pounds, now his running weight was 155 pounds. When he runs a marathon his running weight would be around 145 pounds. As our weight went down so did our times and our training milage went up.Within a few months, we increased our training, mileage, and speed considerably. We were running around 40 to 50 miles per week and getting ready for our first 10K.

I didn't know what a 10K was until I met Tom. If you are like me, a 10K is 10,000 meters, which is equivalent to 6.2 miles. My first 10K was a Kihei run sponsored by the Valley Isle Road Runners (VIRR). I don't remember my exact time, but I think it was in the low 40s. I beat my coach and I finished near the front of the pack. After that Tom and I ran several more 10Ks, and we both improved. One of my more memorable runs was the Iao Valley 10K a run that draws a lot of people, even from Oahu. The first part of this run is relatively flat and then uphill. I recall one of the top runners from Maui was close to 50 yards ahead of me, and as we got into the hills, I started catching him. Near the top of the hill, I passed him. It wasn't long on the downhill, he passed me. However, I was proud of myself, and our time was fairly close. I ran Iao in under 38 minutes. I found out that running up hills was my strength.

Now I could run with Tom and have clean fingers. Our company was up and running. My calluses were gone. Tom had bigger things on his mind, bigger than 10Ks. He wanted us to enter the Maui Marathon. A marathon is 26.22 miles. By this time, we were running 50–60 miles per week. The Maui Marathon was a hard marathon. It had its share of hills, in addition, it was warm. Runners normally do their best in temperatures between 50–60 degrees F, Maui was probably between 70–80 degrees even though it started just after sunrise. It started in Wailuku and ended in Lahaina going over the Pali and through the tunnel to the banyan tree. I figured with the amount of training and my positive mental attitude (PMA); I could finish this marathon in three hours. That would be a 6-minute and 50-second pace for 26.22 miles. A very bold goal for my first marathon. So much for PMAs.

I was on pace for 20 miles, then I hit the wall when I severely struggled with the last 6.2 miles. I remember at one point near the end, a woman runner was catching me and passing me as her cheering section cheered as they drove by. I felt that they were laughing at me. That was rubbing salt in a wound. I finished almost 17 minutes over my expected time of 3 hours. I was disappointed but determined. Tom ran a 3:22 and his goal was 3:20 so he did very well. He concluded that we needed longer training runs. One of our best friends whom we met through running was Bob Folk. He was a good runner, a good trainer, and a lot of fun. He identified himself as the baldheaded midget. We are the same height, but I have more hair. Maybe I should be identified as the hairy midget. The three of us planned a 20 miler around the Kahakuloa side of the island. It is beautiful; however, the road is terrible going up and down the steep slopes of the mountainside and mostly unpaved and hot. Hardly anyone lives out there, except for the people living in this little Hawaiian village, Kahakuloa.

Bob's brother was going to be the escort van driver to provide water and pick us up at the end of the 20 miles and take us back home. He didn't show up at the end. Those were days before cell phones, we were all dehydrated, weary and hot, and frustrated and in addition to that, I was pissed. We did our 20-mile run, plus we walked 4 or 5 more miles. We last saw him around the 15-mile mark and then didn't see him for another two hours. When he finally came I was not in a good mood, I think he was smoking pot. Bob has remained to be one of my closest friends, but his brother I never care to see him again and I don't hold grudges. Bob became a very close friends with our entire family and he is genuine The kids loved him, and they affectionately called him Bill Bill.

Maybe one of the kids forgot his name, but Bill Bill was very appropriate. He has a great sense of humor and loves being with our kids. He is a very down-to-earth person, but when it comes to math, computer sciences, mechanics and so many other things, he is a whiz. He has always been into fitness including weightlifting and yoga. He never married, but he had girlfriends. He lived at our house downstairs for about a year with one girlfriend. That relationship ended but now he is with a wonderful girl in Northern California whom Tom and Young and Evelyn and I plan to visit.

Tom, Bill Bill, and I entered a half-marathon on Thanksgiving Day. It was appropriately called the "Turkey Trot." I won! That was the first and only race that I ever won. I won a turkey. One of my favorite runs was the Tedeschi Vineyard 10K. This run started at Rice Park in Kula. The elevation is about 2800 and the races finished at Tedeschi Vineyard in Ulupalakua 6.2 miles away on a hilly route at about 2000-foot elevation. Tom, Bill Bill, and I set our best personal times (PR). I ran under 35 minutes, Tom broke 38 minutes, and Bill Bill was close behind. The slightly downhill course and cool climate made for ideal running.

Our next marathon was the Kauai Marathon. We took the families and had a great time. I set my goal of a three-hour marathon time again. I felt I had learned from my Maui disappointment and now I had more training, guess what? I broke 3 hours, coming in with 2 hours and 56 minutes. We did many other runs including the Hana Relays in which we assembled a good team. We had Bob Folk, John Smizer, a friend of Tom's from Honolulu, one of John's coworkers, Tom, and me. We each ran four legs of the relay and finished in Hana 52 miles from our start in Wailuku. Each leg averages 2.6 miles. By the fourth leg, your body is wiped out and your muscles are tight and sore. It is not easy running 2.6 miles as fast as you can, then waiting for approximately on hour for your next turn. We did great as a team and finished 3rd overall. Our time of 5 hours and 2 minutes would have won many of the annual Hana Relays. The following year we ran as a family team, Evelyn, Young, Kimberly, Jennifer, Tom, and I were all teammates. We won for having the most fun. We ran in another relay, this one started at sea level and ended thirty-six miles away at the top of Haleakala at an elevation of 10,032 feet. It is called the "Run to the Sun" and has become quite renowned for the ultramarathoners.

The ultramarathoners don't do relays, they run the 36 miles alone competing with other masochists. We were not quite as masochistic with Tom, Bob Folk, and I did it as a relay team. To this date, I don't remember it. Tom had to tell me that we did it. Maybe my brain wants to forget, or I had amnesia.

Tom and I planned a hike for the VIRR. The day before the VIRR event, we hiked into "Swinging Bridges" a trail in upper Waihee that passes over this very wobbly swinging suspension bridge that is elevated about twenty plus feet above the Waihee Stream. At the end of the trail is a waterfall and a deep pond. Tom and I carried a case of beer each and suspended it in the water deep enough to be there for the next day. That was no easy task carrying the beer along a 2.5-mile trail, especially when we got thirsty. When the VIRR members got there, they were pleasantly greeted with a cool beer.

The big boy is coming up. The first week in December is the Honolulu Marathon. Now I had a new goal: 2 hours and 50 minutes. To qualify for the Boston Marathon at my age group, the qualifying time was 2 hours and 50 minutes now it is three hours. I wanted to qualify. My average pace would need to be 6 minutes and 30 seconds per mile for 26.22 miles. I had (PMA) Positive Mental Attitude again. This time my PMA worked. I ran 2 hours, 49 minutes and 46 seconds. I made my goal by 14 seconds and I qualified for Boston. That year I finished 126 out of over 10,000 runners. I was on TV because I collapsed over the finish line. About the last 500 yards, I hit the wall again and started cramping up. I put everything into my effort; I had to continue.

That was my last marathon and my running days were soon to be over. I was training for Boston doing more speed work as I would sprint at full speed, then run, sprint, run faster, more sprinting, less running. After doing speed work my hips started hurting so I went to the doctor for my run-ending diagnosis, osteoarthritis of the hips. That was disappointing news for me and Tom as my running days were some of the best days in my life. After putting up with a lot of pain and discomfort and barely able to get up from the ground after weeding, my doctor and I decided it was time for my hips to be replaced. About ten years had passed since my running days when I had both hips replaced. Tom continued to run. He ran the Hilo Marathon in 3 hours and 12 minutes and was in the top 50 and made the Hilo news. We still got together a lot but not as much as before. I missed running with him, but we would still drink beer together. Eventually, after I healed from my hip surgeries we started walking together along with Evelyn, Young, and our dogs. We have been walking together for nearly thirty years. Our times have slowed over the years. Our wives set their pace and walk about 2½ miles five days a week and Tom and I walk three miles six days a week. Tom is approaching seventy-eight and is a vegan. He swore off drinking beer but that doesn't prevent him from drinking it. He had a minor heart attack a few years back and now is extremely health conscious.

One of my vivid memories during our running days didn't occur while I was running, it occurred because of my driving. I was driving toward my house on Waiehu Beach Road when I heard a siren. I proceeded into my subdivision and pulled into my driveway. The siren was still going, and I was the reason.

A rotund policeman got out of his car and said, "Why didn't you stop?!!"

I told him that I didn't think he was going after me. He said, "You were speeding!"

I said, "What!!!?"

In an unmannerly voice, he said, "You were speeding; I want to see your driver's license." I told him I wasn't speeding as I proceeded to pull out my driver's license. His tone was offensive as I gave my license to the officer.

He looked at it and said in a demeaning tone, "Where are your glasses?"

I said, in a demeaning tone, "I wear contacts," I proceeded to take one out on this windy day and the contact blew off my finger. I was pissed! Then I looked at the officer and said, "You would do much better at your job if you lost fifty pounds." I was at the peak of my marathon training at the time weighing 143 lbs. with a BMI of 18.5 and I was buff. I estimated his BMI to be close to 30, which is obese. I could have run away from him but decided not to. He quickly put me in handcuffs. If I was black, I would be dead. He put me in the back of his squad car, pushed my head down as Trump suggests, and took me to the police station for booking. On the way to the police station, I saw Dick Fukushima, my main competitor, in a truck next to me as I crunched down hoping he didn't see me. At the police station I was booked for unruly behavior. I just gave the officer some deserving advice and yet I had to get bailed out jail. My bail was set at $100. I had to use a pay telephone at the station to call Tom to bail me out as I chose not to call Evelyn.

My court appearance was in about three weeks. At that time, the chief of police was Chief Tavares, and my arresting officer was Officer Tavares. Guess what, they are father and son. I didn't know what was going to happen in court and I was concerned. With Evelyn by my side, we saw Doug Samashima, a lawyer I knew approaching us. He quietly asked if I would allow the case just to drop. I was in shock. I agreed, but in retrospect, I should have only agreed to drop it if Officer Tavares agreed to lose 50 pounds. A few years later he was fired from the force.

CHAPTER 18

Our Children Growing Up 1977–1986

Evelyn and the kids were doing great, she was, and still is, a super mom. As the kids were growing up, I could be a bit impatient. I could make them feel uncomfortable at the dinner table, criticizing their table manners. Mom's impatience rubbed off on me. All three children went to the Hongwanji preschool where Mrs. Oishi was an excellent administrator. She and Miss Kay were so caring and kind. The kids loved it, and it was so nice for Evelyn to get a break. The staff loved our kids as Evelyn always had them prepared and on time for school. The school was disciplined and structured as the kids would remove their shoes before going into the classroom. When they take naps, there was not a squeak but when they were in the playground you couldn't hear yourself think. We have Jeff's graduation picture from Hongwanji in a collage in our bedroom. What a great start for them getting ready for Waihee Elementary School. As a family, we were always together with Pizza Hut our favorite meal out. Evelyn would cook almost every night, except for Pizza Hut night. If we went to the Delmore's. she would always bring a dish. Other close friends at that time included Jim and Sonya Hayes, older neighbors who lived up the street. We would often have friends over for Evelyn's great cooking on the weekends.

I would read to the kids at night and get impatient with them just because of my nature, just like my mom and I would check their homework. I was kind of the school dad. Evelyn had a calming effect on the kids. She was the planner, cook, and the rock. She supported me in decision-making, except when I was wrong, which was most of the time. Evelyn was a super mom whom they could confide in.

As the kids grew up, they got into more and more activities. Jennifer played soccer and always has been a fitness buff. I remember one soccer game in Lahaina. it had rained during the day and was drizzling at game time. Jennifer was all muddy at its conclusion. The only part of her that wasn't muddy was her shiny white teeth behind her big smile. She was my hero. Jennifer played a super game. Jennifer was becoming a beauty. She wasn't as outgoing as Jill, but she had a beautiful disposition and plenty of friends. Lisa Giamoris is the first to come to mind. Lisa was smart, wacky, and sometimes very wacky and just fun to be around I. have always enjoyed Lisa very much. Their personalities were a good match. Jennifer was more on the reserved side than wacky Lisa.

Jeff was good at sports, although young and small, he could hold his own. He tried out for Little League when he was of age. I took him down to the Wailuku ball fields, and to my disappointment, he was cut along with several others, because there were too many kids trying out for the number of teams they had. Jeff, being small and a late born was at a disadvantage. He tried out for the White Sox but was cut from the team. I was disappointed. I checked on starting a new team when he was cut. There was a baseball field in Waihee that wasn't being used and it had everything we needed. I talked to the commissioner, and he said we could proceed if we could get enough players. That wasn't a problem. We got all the inexperienced players that were cut from the White Sox. None of our players had ever played a game before. Mark Mizuno, John Umeno, and I coached the kids. I think I was the head coach.

We had fun with the kids as they learned the fundamentals of baseball and we enjoyed their parents, but we hated the umpires, who doesn't when you play baseball. We had a perfect season, losing every game we played. One of my favorite players was "Homerun Higgens." He was on the chubby side and if he was fortunate to hit the ball, by the time he got to first base his pants were around his knees. It was so funny to watch him run, but he had a very good disposition as did all the players. Jeff was good at catching the ball and making proper field decisions but wasn't a great hitter his first year. There was a considerable improvement from our first practice to our last. It was always a family event going to the games.

We always had a ping-pong table. Evelyn and I loved to play. Jeff would patiently wait his turn and he got better quickly. I had no mercy with him and I would skunk him if I could. But he was getting better and it was only a matter of a couple of years before he got to the point of beating me on occasions. Then a few more years where he could skunk me. When he started beating me all the time, I didn't want to play with him anymore. In addition to being a good athlete, Jeff was musically inclined. He learned to play the piano and he was good. We have a beautiful grand piano in our living room, and I thought it was going to be a piece of furniture, but Jeff brought it to life. Dr. Doug was Jeff's piano teacher. He was a great teacher, and Jeff enjoyed him. He was not the typical piano teacher. He liked "rock" and "Piano Man" and fast-moving music and so did Jeff. Jeff would practice for hours between lessons and in short order, he was playing the Turkish March over and over again, until he perfected it. Jeff had the touch and the ear for music. He became very good and provided a lot of entertainment for us. He could do no wrong for Evelyn, but it was very hard to get him to rake leaves for me. He hated yard work and he still does, saying it is because of me. Jeff has a calming nature and is not impatient like me.

Jill could get a little rambunctious at times. Jill enjoyed the hula and was and still is a very graceful dancer. She got that from her mother. Evelyn surprised me with a beautiful solo hula at our wedding as Jill did at her wedding. At a young age, Jill was also a good writer. She may have been in the sixth grade, and I read one of her poems. I accused her of plagiarism. She couldn't have written it. It was too good. I wanted the truth and the truth to me was plagiarism so I insisted until I made her cry. I was furious because lying was not in my playbook. I was wrong; what a poopy dad I was. I felt terrible as I got a big scolding from Evelyn. Jill was also very creative. She and her friend Sierra Wolfson used our video camera to record a skit out of the clear blue sky.

It was so good and so funny. Evelyn and I watched it several times; and then we think we erased it by mistake; we wish we could watch that recording again. Jill was a big part of our advertising for Maui Fumigation. When she was ten years old, we centered our advertising around her where we did primarily radio and newspaper advertising. I would write out something catchy about termites and ants or the like and she would say it on air. The DJs were impressed, "Take One" and it was perfect. She was not only good she was great. She may have done around twenty radio spots for us, and she was in the newspaper nearly every week.

However, when she turned eleven years old, she retired because kids referred to her as the "termite girl" and she didn't like that.

All three of our kids were good students and were on the honor rolls. They had no special gift of superintelligence, but they were blue-collar; they worked hard at their studies.

We did take some trips with the children in those days. We primarily went to visit my family in California and Evelyn's family in Honolulu. Our earliest vacation with our kids was to Yosemite. Jennifer was almost two and Jill was in the basket. I wanted to show Evelyn its beauty and grandeur. As a kid, I had fond memories of Yosemite. We took Mommy and Daddy. They had never been on a vacation in their life other than visiting relatives. Daddy was fun to travel with. He was excited to see the sights, he called Yosemite, "Yo-so-mi-ti. As we looked at El Capitan, there was snow on the ground and the sun reflecting off this granite monolith. It was breathtaking, reminding me of his statement, "I can see my breath," as he exhaled in the cold weather. Mommy was so easy to travel with and Jennifer and Jill did fine. That was a great trip.

When our kids were old enough to travel, we took them on more trips to the mainland. One of our earlier trips was to visit Oregon and Washington. Jennifer was probably six, Jill three, and Jeff may have been in diapers. In Oregon, we went to St. Helens and visited Norman and Nadine Ichimura and their kids. They were early friends of ours when we first moved to Maui. Norman was an engineer working for Pioneer Mill in Lahaina. Nadine was from Oregon and wanted to go back. Norman was able to get a good job as an engineer in the paper mill in St. Helens. They invited us to visit, so we did. St. Helens, being a paper mill town, had a very distinct smell. It stank. I guess one would get used to it if you lived there, but I never got used to it. We drove to Camas, Washington to visit Cely, Evelyn's cousin, and her husband Doug and their son Ryan who was a good golfer. I pulled out one of his drivers and asked him to watch me swing.

I said, "I think it is pretty good."

He reluctantly said, "That's a terrible swing." Oh well, I didn't like golf anyway.

A trip that Evelyn and I took with the kids was to British Columbia, Canada. I met two contractors working on a reconstruction project at the Maui Lu. They were from Vancouver. BC. and suggested that I come up and I did, wife, kids, and all. The thing I remember most was it was the coldest I have ever been in my entire life. I have always lived in a warm climate, Southern California and Hawaii. With only a windbreaker in nineteen-degree windy weather, I froze. This gave me a lot of respect for my friend Tom, who grew up in Wisconsin where the temperature can go -20F.

Mommy asked us to take her to the Philippines. The kids were too young to go. Ester was so gracious to watch them in our absence. The flight from Hawaii is very long. I think we flew for eleven hours in Economy. When we arrived in Manila we were in fair shape when greeted by Evelyn's cousins, Junior and Bobot. They picked us up in an older Mercedes. We stayed in Manila for a few days where Evelyn was concerned about my well-being since I was an easy target for pickpockets or even gangsters. She has a good imagination. Junior and Bobot stayed by my side the whole time. Junior was a retiree from the military and Bobot was a policeman in Manila. I was well protected, although I was probably safer in the Philippines than I would be in the United States today. In Manila, to drive, you must have your hand on the horn because honking is required. The honking and the noise of the motorbikes were deafening in Manila, a very busy city. Bobot, being a policeman, got special favors when he showed his badge and that kind of bothered me. The majority of people in Manila speaks Tagalog. There are over 100 different dialects in the Philippines. Evelyn can understand Tagalog but doesn't feel comfortable speaking it since her dialect is Ilocano.

Junior drove us in the Mercedes from Manila to Laoag, which is about a nine-hour drive on pretty good roads. In Laoag, they speak Ilocano. Laoag is the capitol city of the province of Ilocos Norte, the northernmost province in the Philippines, and in this province is where the majority of Filipino sugarcane and pineapple workers came to Hawaii from. Evelyn has several relatives in Laoag. Some of my memories include watching the ladies wash their clothes in the Laoag River. Why do I remember this? They were bare-breasted. I could fish there for hours if Evelyn would let me. She wouldn't.

Evelyn says this is not true and that I have a good imagination. She could be right. We stayed one night at Fort Ilocandia a five-star hotel with excellent service and accommodations. There is a casino at the hotel that has a different atmosphere than Las Vegas; it is much more relaxed. From Laoag, we went to

Dingras, where Daddy was born along with his twelve siblings and Evelyn in a bamboo house with no water or electricity. Dingras is just over a one-hour drive from Laoag where we visited Evelyn's relatives and saw the carabao in the fields. The pace of life in Dingras was on the opposite end of the spectrum from Manila. From Dingras we took a bus to Baguio, the city where Evelyn was raised until she was eleven years old. The bus would make many stops along the way with one stop confusing me. The bus driver yelled out "Isbu" and stopped. Everyone got off the bus and I noticed all the ladies squatting and all the men going pee. I found out that was the restroom stop. There were no facilities but who needs a facility? We stayed at the Pines Hotel near Monette's house, Evelyn's closest relative by friendship, although they don't know how they are related. Having just moved from Baguio to Daly City, California, Monette was not there. We met her brother, Ed, holding a cock. Not his cock, a cock, I mean a male chicken. He raises cocks, no, that doesn't sound good either. Cockfighting is the favorite sport of the Philippines Although I haven't seen that in the Olympics yet. Baguio has a great climate but has changed considerably since Evelyn was born. It was a much smaller city then. Now it has a population of over 340,000. We had a great trip and we knew we would return. When we got back to Maui, the kids were happy to see us and so was Ester.

One year we took the kids to see my family in California, and after a short visit, we met Bill Bill at the Grand Canyon on a fun and educational family vacation. Bill Bill is not only my friend; he became a great friend of the family. We joined him in Arizona for a tremendous tour of the Grand Canyon. We all enjoyed it so much and we enjoyed Bill Bill's navigation skills in his motor home and his wonderful sense of humor.

One vacation we took together with the kids was fun for me. We didn't go to Disneyland or Knotts Berry Farm as was their wish. We did briefly see my family, which they always enjoyed, then we went looking for water lily businesses. I grew a deep passion for water gardens. In the process of landscaping my yard, I built four ponds and planted them with water lilies, lotus, and other aquatic plants. I did a lot of research, and the ponds came out beautiful. I was intense, as I wanted to learn as much as I could about water gardening. Before our trip, I found that there were two water garden companies I wanted to visit while in California. One was in Santa Barbara and another in Napa. These two locations are a long distance from each other. I loved the trip, the kids didn't. Evelyn was neutral.

Generally, we would visit my family in the Los Angeles area on an annual basis and sometimes go to Daly City, near San Francisco to see Monette and take side trips. One year my side trips included water gardens. I was so intrigued with water lilies and aquatic plants because of my first water garden. After visiting my family, we drove to Santa Barbara Water Gardens and I spoke to Virginia Hayes, its owner. It was a small business, growing, selling, and maintaining water lilies, lotus, and other aquatic plants. Virginia knew a lot about aquatic plants, and I wanted to learn. I asked her if I could work with her for a week and if she would be my mentor. She agreed so we made the arrangements. The plan was for me to come back in about three months without Evelyn and the kids to learn water gardening. On that same trip, we went to visit Monette in Daly City. I was anxious to go to Napa, California to visit another water garden company. The name of the company was McAlister's Water Gardens, and the owner was Walt McAllister. He had a very interesting operation growing all of his waterlilies in small pots rather than ponds. It was very organized, and he seemed to be very professional. I just googled him, and his business has survived. I did go back to Santa Barbara and worked with Virginia and learned a lot about aquatic plants, including water lilies, lotus, and many others.

Our kids were fun to grow up with. On the whole, we enjoyed growing up together except for when I was impatient. They generally got along well and seemed quite content with life on Maui. Of the three, there wasn't a brat like me to my four sisters.

CHAPTER 19

Business Headaches 1986

Our business was growing but not making much profit. A relatively new company owned by Mike was affecting our bottom line. I will leave it at that. He hit it off well with me from the onset because I interviewed him for a job that he had no intention of taking. He just wanted to get information about our company. He already had his paperwork in to the state to start his business. He did many, many sneaky things which isn't typical Maui business style, but Mike, being from New Jersey, brought a new style to Maui. I am sure there are good companies in New Jersey and he was the exception. He would speak nicely in front of you and then stab you in the back. He eventually got into fumigation and priced his estimates much lower than ours and got his share of the business, and he grew rapidly. He was aggressive, knowledgeable, cheap, and sneaky and a constant pain until he sold his business to a Fortune 500 Company many years later. This Fortune 500 had purchased several Oahu Pest Control companies and now was fishing for Maui companies.

My conservative business style was changing. Evelyn and I went to a National Pest Control Convention and there I met with some of my former Texas pest control customers. Two very successful companies to which I sold chemicals, told me about their experiences with TADD dogs. TADD dogs were trained beagles to sniff out termites. The owner of TADD would train a person in the participating termite company to properly use the dogs. The TADD dogs would alert the handler when they came across termites. The two companies that I met at National gave me positive feedback about the TADD program. Even though Hawaii had a six-month quarantine law for dogs I decided to employ the TADD program. Clem was our designated handler, and he worked with our dog at the quarantine station in Honolulu.

At the time we negotiated for our TADD dog, I was talked into having two TADD dogs. We would pay Bob, the owner $25,000 per year for each dog for his fee. That did not include the care and maintenance of the dog, our office expenses, payroll, etc. We would have one dog for Oahu and one for Maui. We hired Candice to be our Oahu handler while Clem would be on Maui. Our justification for two dogs was due to Hawaii's six-month quarantine. If our dog died, got sick, or became ineffective, Bob would replace it. New dogs entering Hawaii were quarantined for six months so if you built your business around one dog and something happened, your business would suffer. We opened our office on Oahu. Clem, Candice and I opened the office. Candice's dog was still in quarantine. She would go out with Clem on inspections in addition to working with her dog in quarantine. I think we worked for less than one month on Oahu and I realized something was very wrong. I began having a lot of anxiety and I couldn't concentrate and sleep. I was going through my first of many bipolar depression bouts. We closed the Oahu office abruptly and I came back to Maui with my tail between my legs. I couldn't work and I couldn't function. I was manic when planning the TADD dog fiasco. After a manic stage, depression followed. I was forty years old at the time. The average time for the onset of bipolar symptoms is in the midtwenties.

This was in 1988 and Jeff was starting his second year in baseball. I couldn't coach because I was spending most of my time on Oahu. When I got back, the team was doing well although I wasn't. At that time we were in the process of building a new house not far from where we lived, mortgage rates were very high, over 10%. We sold our house on an agreement of sale, meaning we would carry the note. We rented a house in our subdivision, hopefully until our house was built. We had to foreclose on the buyer of our home because they went into default and we never got paid. We had to go to court to get our house back. It took forever. It was a financially stressful time in addition to the TADD dog fiasco. When I returned from Oahu I didn't return to work for a while. I was suffering from major anxiety and depression. I stayed away from Maui Fumigation because I couldn't concentrate, so I had to take time off. I sought psychiatric help. One psychiatrist,

I saw shared an office with four other doctors and he was in a back corner room, which was very messy. We talked and I tried to explain my symptoms. One of his statements was something like, "Some would have committed suicide by now."

This didn't sit well with me so told my family doctor, Dr. Kwon, what was said. He immediately referred me to another psychiatrist. I was very frustrated with many of the psychiatrists that I saw. I was suicidal however I could drive. but I felt like I was in a fog of confusion. At that time, I thought it would be easy to drive in front of a great big semitruck to get out of my misery or if I was at a tall building, I could jump and it would be over. I was miserable and it seemed there was no solution however, if I committed suicide Evelyn would be devastated. Evelyn was my salvation. I thought of her every time I had suicidal thoughts and I promised to myself that I would never take my life by suicide. I loved Evelyn and our three kids. So many depressed people do not have an Evelyn. Fortunately, I did. The medications weren't working, and I felt like a zombie. Over time I would very gradually return to normal. I have gone through depression on multiple occasions, this first one was one of the worst. I wasn't very functional for approximately three months although Evelyn was there for me.

CHAPTER 20

Our New House, Vicky, and Water Gardens 1988–2001

As our house was nearing completion, I was getting better. My anxiety was on the decline, and I was starting to have some more energy and my thoughts were turning more positive. Was I well enough to paint my house? I have painted every house I have owned. I hadn't gone to work for a couple of months, mostly staying in the bedroom and still not quite ready to go back. Our house is an architecturally designed, two-story house with five bedrooms and three baths, consisting of approximately 2800 square feet. It has an ocean view and a flowing stream as its rear boundary. I did start painting and I was gradually feeling better. Hour by hour, day by day, I was becoming myself once again. I painted every square inch of our house, inside and out by myself. It made Evelyn nervous as I had to be on some tall ladders but it came out great and by the time I finished, my depression was gone. We found a new buyer for our Waiehu Heights house, and everything was looking better but I still wasn't ready to go back to work, not because of my depression. I just wasn't ready.

The business was running quite smoothly without me. After painting the house, I decided to landscape the yard. We have about 18,000 square feet of land. Our terrain is a big slope from the front of the lot to the back where it meets the Waiehu Stream. I wanted to make the yard beautiful, but I knew it was beyond my ability. I contacted my "Big Brother" John Herr, from my fraternity, a Cal Poly graduate, Landscape Architect. I knew he could help me. I told John I would pay for the airfare for him, his wife, Suzanne, and daughter, Ashley to fly to Maui. They could stay at our new home, in return for drawings to landscape my yard. He took me up on it and he did a great job. Near the stream is a putting green with a winding walking path from the back of our drive. I built the rock retaining walls, which consist of more than 110 tons of rock. I probably spent nearly five months building the walls. I did everything and was completely depression-free. I installed the sprinkler system, which was a pain in the butt, and put in a gazebo and four ponds for my waterlilies. Ten months earlier, I was considering suicide.

One afternoon as I was working on the rock walls, Evelyn came down and told me that one of our employees had embezzled quite a bit of money from us. Sande, our superstar office manager, figured out Vickie's scheme and Sande could account for $32,000 that was stolen, there may have been more. I continued working on the rock wall. Owning a business can be stressful. When I was working in the yard, I didn't feel any stress. No, I shouldn't say that. Putting in the sprinkler system caused stress.

Vickie was another case. She was smart and cunning in her mid-thirties, large-breasted and flirtatious. Her husband, Rick worked with us, and Vickie joined us later. She worked with us for probably four or five years. We fumigate for a lot of Filipino homeowners, and at that time they generally paid in cash. Vickie would delete the account and keep the money. Simple. I wasn't paying attention to the Profit and Loss Statements (P&Ls) because I was enjoying my lack of stress. If I were working, I may have caught it. We fired her and advised her to hire an attorney because we were going to take her to court. In the meantime, she and Rick moved to Oregon.

Before the hearing before the judge, she was extradited to Hawaii and had to stay in prison for a few days. At the court hearing, she pleaded "No Contest." The judge ruled in our favor and ordered her to pay $150 per month until her debt was resolved. With our legal fees, this amount would take over twenty-two years to pay off. We got about $1,500 and then the payments stopped and we couldn't find her. Was it worth it for us to look? We won but we lost. Many years later I got a call from her husband Rick, asking me that we reopen the case with Vicky. They had divorced and she took everything she could from him, and she embezzled another employer. Did she learn her lesson? It's a real gamble with the court system and I am batting below average. I am not like Trump.

The landscaping was finished, and I was watching things grow. When I ordered the waterlilies for the four ponds, I ordered them through a mail-order catalog, because I couldn't get any locally. I paid approximately $35 per waterlily, and I ordered ten. I ordered other aquatic plants, a couple of pumps, and filters and by the time I was finished, I spent close to $1,000. By the next year, my ponds were overgrown with beautiful water lilies. It was time to re-pot. As I started separating the lilies; I realized this one plant had five new water lilies. My mind quickly did the math. 5 X $35 X 10 = $3,500. Hey, I can make money at this. I was starting to get manic. I wasn't thinking of selling the water lilies from my four small ponds at my home. I wanted big ponds. We owned a two-acre parcel of land with a house on it in Peahi.

It had plenty of land to build ponds. I told Dick Price, our pest control manager for Maui Fumigation, my idea which he jumped on it like a fly on ****. He talked to a friend who had built ponds before and discussed my idea. I was manic when all these grandiose ideas entered my head about making lots of money selling waterlilies. I had double hip surgery at the time to replace my arthritic hips. I was in the hospital and Dick Price visited. We discussed the pond project. We were going to put in two ponds, approximately 2,000 square feet each but he told me he dug seven ponds of that size. There would be a considerable expense to line the ponds and stock them. My manic idea grew into a headache. Now depression and anxiety were starting to set in.

We grew some beautiful water lilies which we sold to the hotels and many homeowners. They bought our products including pond liners, pumps, aquatic plants, and waterlilies. Our cost of doing business was more than what we were making. Maui Fumigation had to cover its expenses. Water Gardens of Hawaii never went anywhere and at one time we opened a retail outlet near Maui Fumigation, but my depression got in the way. Evelyn worked very hard at Water Gardens of Hawaii along with Gloria and Caro, but it wasn't in the cards. Water Gardens of Hawaii was started when I was manic and ended when I was depressed.

Dr. Tom Seif, Tom to me and everyone else, a very good friend of mine and Evelyn, was our go-to person for our computers for the office. This was about 1992. Tom, a psychologist, converted his intelligence to computers as he was a big help to Maui Fumigation. He approached me with his new idea to make money. It was to sell jewelry with a company called JewelWay. He presented their marketing plan and it intrigued me. Evelyn loves jewelry so she was excited. We had a JewelWay party at our house to which we invited a lot of our friends and it was a smashing success. Almost everyone there bought jewelry and were energized about selling it. Our marketing plan was working and our network was growing. We were going to make money and I was getting manic. We were planning a trip to California to see my family so perfect, we'll plan to have a JewelWay meeting in California with family and friends.

Kip came to see us but was not interested in staying for the JewelWay presentation. I was upset because I was manic and I was so sure this was the perfect way for him to make money. Kip and I lost touch for many years after that. He lived in California for a while longer but eventually went to Costa Rica where he settled down. The JewelWay meeting went well. Patty purchased the most, spending $2,000, Pam and Bonnie also purchased jewelry. When we returned to Maui, Tom was hustling me to have another JewelWay party. My manic mode had fizzled, depression was quickly approaching and as it did, I went into my depression shell. JewelWay was a dream of the past. In 1997, the Federal Trade Commission (FTC) asserted that the JewelWay was an illegal pyramid scheme. JewelWay International, Inc. and its corporate officers were required to pay $5,000,000 to be distributed to harmed consumers and provisions halting the challenged conduct. *www.ftc.gov. Oh well, just another bipolar episode.

(Note: Kip and I recently got back in touch and Evelyn and I are planning to see him in Costa Rica at the end of the year.)

CHAPTER 21

Jen and Gary 1994–1995

I had become the President of the Hawaii Pest Control Association. The title might sound impressive but Tim Lyons, the owner of the management company that manages our association does all the work. I was a figurehead. One of the perks of being president was a paid trip for two to the National Pest Control Convention. That year it was going to be in Orlando, Florida. Tim found out that there was an International Pest Convention that year in Hong Kong. I said I would rather go to Hong Kong and the board approved it. Evelyn and I had a wonderful time except for the last day. We got a call from Freddy, our nephew, who was staying with our kids while we were gone. Freddie informed us that Jennifer had written a note letting us know she was pregnant and that she had run away and for no one to go after her or something would happen. That shook both of us up, especially Evelyn. Jennifer was fourteen years old and had a seventeen-year-old, irresponsible boyfriend, Gary. Gary probably weighed around 130 pounds and was rather scrawny and not real bright.

We couldn't see what Jen saw in him. He got one other young girl pregnant before Jennifer. The flight from Hong Kong home was torturous. We found that Jennifer was staying with Gary at his parent's house, a rather dysfunctional household. When we got home, we didn't know what to do. Her cheerleading coach, Joanne Yap was in close contact with Jennifer and was our go-between. Jen was mixed up and being very independent, made things more difficult. She was beautiful, with a body of an eighteen-year-old and she was fourteen, which made this harder. She was not attending her classes at Saint Anthony, a Catholic school, where she was on the honor roll and a cheerleader. We spoke with Sister Leone at her school who informed us that Jennifer was close to being kicked out.

Sister Leone is a warm, compassionate person and was one of Jennifer's teachers. All of Jen's friends and teachers were very concerned about her. How did this young girl change so quickly from a loving daughter to a rebellious disconnect? She didn't want to see her family, Jill, Jeff and Evelyn, and myself. We knew she needed some time, and we gave that to her, but now it has been too long. Over a month had passed and Evelyn and I were so concerned and so worried. Thoughts of "Did we fail as parents?" filled our heads. Jill and Jeff didn't know what to make of it as we looked at each other with blank stares at the dinner table. I am not sure why, but Jennifer did come home. There was still a lot of tension when Jen came home. I remember one time, the three of us, Jennifer, Evelyn, and myself were in a discussion and it got heated. Jennifer swore at Evelyn with degrading vulgar language. I slapped her face hard. That wasn't like me, I didn't hit the kids and it wasn't like Jen.

What is happening? I felt bad. How did this get to this point? Jennifer called the police to report that I slapped her. Nothing resulted from the police report; however, my quick temper took over when she swore at her mother who loved her so much. I gave Jen a black eye and her face swelled. Fortunately, things calmed down somewhat. We would allow Gary to come to our house and be with Jen, however, Evelyn and I were uncomfortable. Jennifer began attending classes again and she maintained her grades and resumed school with little interference. At this point, Evelyn and I did not know what to do with Jennifer. She was still very indifferent. We were getting advice from family, our friends, and from her school on what we should do about the unborn baby. She was approaching three months in her pregnancy, and we had three choices. Let Jennifer keep the child, put it up for adoption, or abortion. Jennifer wanted to keep the child and Evelyn and I were leaning more toward adoption or abortion.

After some very worrisome days and nights, we chose abortion. There was no way Jennifer was old enough and mature enough to be a good mother. Gary, already fathering one other child and providing no support, was not ready to be a good dad. Ester, Evelyn's sister, was the nurse for Dr. Kushi, Evelyn's and Jennifer's gynecologist on Maui and was very good and respected. Evelyn and Ester talked to Dr. Kushi about the abortion procedure and asked if he could do it. By now Jennifer was three months pregnant. He didn't want to do it himself so he referred us to a Honolulu doctor. The arrangements were made. Violet, our niece, was to pick up Jennifer at the Honolulu airport and take her to the hospital. I was to take Jennifer to the Maui airport. Jennifer got into my car very reluctantly. The moment we got out of our driveway she was crying and as we drove farther, she started getting louder and crying more, sobbing "I don't want to, I don't want to," over and over again. I love Jennifer, I can't force her to do this. After driving about two miles I turned the car around and headed home. When I got home, Ester and Evelyn were confused.

"What happened?"

I said, "We're going to have a baby." That decision and proposing to Evelyn were the two best decisions I have ever made in my life.

There were still tough times ahead. We tried to help Jen and Gary. They tried to earn a little extra spending money by working at our waterlily farm. Jennifer is a hard worker, but Gary was lazy. We had them also clean the office once a week. Not too long after that Gary was caught breaking into our office stealing money. We didn't see Gary much after that and neither did Jen. We were so relieved that their relationship ended.

CHAPTER 22

The End of a Family Business 1976–1991

Maui Fumigation grew to approximately twenty employees by 1991 and we were doing around $1.5 million in annual revenue. Maui Fumigation became an excellent fumigation company. We did one of the largest fumigations ever done on Maui. The building at 250 Alamaha in Kahului was 1.4 million cubic feet. That is equivalent to forty-seven, three-bedroom, one-bath houses with a garage, for one fumigation. This building was covered in four days. We purchased over $20,000 for additional tarps to cover this building. That was a lot of money in those days. We certainly did not want a blowout on this structure and fortunately the fumigation went well.

We had a lot of dedicated employees who worked hard on the job. Rumors started that the same Fortune 500 company that was purchasing other pest control companies in Hawaii was interested in talking to us and the rumors did eventually turn out true. After considerable negotiating, we did sell our business to this Fortune 500 company. We weren't looking for a buyer, but they made us a very nice offer. They paid a down payment and the rest over seven years to hold us to a non-compete contract. The sale of our business came with some excitement. One of our key employees tried to prevent us from selling at the last minute. He got several of the employees together for a boycott and threatened to quit. The deal was already inked, so it wouldn't have voided the purchase. It did cause excitement. This Fortune 500 company had good benefits and they were going to maintain the same wages for our employees. The employees who chose to stay were willing to try. Initially, when in discussion regarding the purchase, I was planning to leave after the purchase and "beat a dead dog with a stick," and revive Water Gardens.

The economy was cooling off and I got cold feet. I offered my services to the buying company. They wanted me to continue managing. For some reason, I was starting another stage of depression. I couldn't concentrate and anxiety was starting to take over. There were some management manuals that I was required to read but I couldn't. I couldn't concentrate. I told my new boss about my depression and recommended that Clem be the branch manager.

They agreed. Clem, reluctant at first, took the job and I became a sales representative. Sales were my preferred choice. I enjoyed diagnosing pest problems and providing solutions. This depression was mild and short-lived. During my employment, my State of Hawaii, Pest Control Operator's License was used for legal purposes for the Maui branch. I was okay with that if they complied with the laws. While Clem was the manager, we complied, and he ran the business as we ran Maui Fumigation. Clem would ignore some of the mainland instructions and would take the heat for it. Eventually, Clem had to step down and as he did, management styles started changing. Many of the old Maui Fumigation employees were getting frustrated, including myself. It was no longer a family-run business and wasn't fun.

This Fortune 500 company-operated significantly differently than our family-run business. Their main concern was the bottom line with customer and employee relations on the wane. Compliance with our licensing laws was not their priority. To sell pest control, termite, or fumigation work in Hawaii, the employee must be licensed. I was always strict holding to our licensing laws. They hired many full-time unlicensed salespeople and as time moved on, more and more unlicensed sales personnel were being hired. I was getting the run-around from our branch manager and the district manager regarding licensing. My license was in jeopardy, and I wasn't getting the facts and they were committing many violations using my license. I saw Luis, Clem's brother, and Mae, visibly upset in the warehouse one afternoon. Luis and I had worked together for over twenty years and Mae worked with me for over eleven years. Mae expressed her concerns.

"They don't show us any respect." Luis, who was Service Manager of the Year for the entire company consisting of close to 10,000 employees, had the same sentiments.

"We're going to quit."

I quickly said, "If you guys are going to quit, I am going to quit also." We were fed up. I said, "I can start a new business." I will work on a business plan to include all of us including Clem. Luis, Mae, and I turned in our resignation letters. In the letter, I was upfront and told them that we were going to start a business. The three of us worked for this subsidiary for ten years. On the day of the acquisition of Maui Fumigation, all employees had to sign a non-compete agreement stating that they cannot compete within 100 miles of the last branch where they were employed, for two years. Luis and Mae signed a revised version that excluded them.

I signed a seven-year non-compete when Maui Fumigation was acquired and now it is ten years later. I did not recall signing this employment agreement. However, they were quick to show me that I did. Everyone in the company signed it. If they were a new hire secretary, they would be required to sign it. It is simply an anticompetition form. I researched it and this form is not enforceable in most states. The companies' attorneys threatened me with court, but I wasn't afraid. I was becoming manic and very confident. Sure enough, I was served with a summons to appear in court. They called my bluff so I hired a Maui attorney, David Jorgenson. He was young, smart, energetic, and optimistic. I liked him a lot but we had a problem. He was going to be in Philadelphia at the time of my hearing. I had to hire another attorney so I chose Bill Nagel who had worked with the Hawaii Pest Control Association on legal matters.

He was Dave Jorgenson's opposite. He was older, not so smart, low energy, and pessimistic. I made a big mistake. My reasoning, why I was hopeful of winning this case was: 1. Is it legal to prevent competition? If so, 2. Is it legal for a company to use my licenses to perform illegal work, and in doing so take my livelihood away? Bill told me I was comparing apples and oranges. We appeared in court and Bill was so nervous, he didn't prepare properly. The Fortune 500 company lawyers were prepared. They made it sound like I was their company's top employee and over the ten years, I had learned all their trade secrets and I was going to steal all their business.

The outcome was somewhat predictable with Mr. Nagel as my attorney. The judge required that we arbitrate. I lost in the fact that I had to cover the attorney fees to my former company. That amounted to over $25,000. But we won in the fact that we could continue in business. We had to agree not to call on any of their customer for two years. We were required to instruct our office staff to screen all calls and to inform the caller if they had used our former employee services in the past two years, we could not provide our services. This upset a lot of former customers, backfiring on them.

I submitted a copy of their recent state sales report to the Department of Commerce and Consumer Affairs (DCCA). I was able to show their sales numbers by the employee and if they were licensed or unlicensed. The majority were not licensed. My report to DCCA generated a considerable amount of investigation. When it was complete, our former employer had to pay a fine of $58,000. At that time, it was the largest fine levied by DCCA against a company in Hawaii. However, fines for large companies are just a slap on the wrist. It is figured in their cost of doing business. The complaints against our former employer were mounting nationwide. One of their distraught customers created a website strictly for complaints against them. I missed the family business style and values. I had enough of the big corporate style.

CHAPTER 23

Starting Bowman Termite 2001–Present

Bowman Termite and Pest Management was operating before the court hearing with our previous employer, not knowing what was going to be the outcome of the case. I was optimistic and yet somewhat realistic. Evelyn and I, Mae, Luis, and Clem, who just joined us, started the company. As I worked on the business plan, I had a hard time with ownership. Evelyn and I would put up the front money and they were to get a share of the business for their loyalty. My attorney advised me that it wasn't a good plan. I struggled with it and procrastinated. I eventually agreed to buy them out rather than making them partners.

Our former employer was putting pressure on us. We put the business in Evelyn's name, and I took a leave of absence. I was the main sales force behind the company. I left the business in the hands of four extremely capable people without the main salesperson, so we limped along. My tactic didn't work. I was starting to feel my manic mood. I decided to get a real estate license and joined my good friend, Tom Delmore at Delmore Realty. I took the Maui real estate course online and passed the exam in five days. When I filled out my application for my license, there was a question on the form—"Are you in a pending lawsuit? I answered yes. When the Board of Realtors got my application, my answer of yes, was a red flag. They contacted me and asked for clarification. There was an upcoming board meeting that I had to attend in Honolulu, there I explained at the board meeting about my lawsuit with my previous employer.

I explained what the lawsuit was regarding. My license was approved. I started working with Tom and checking in the Bowman Termite office periodically. We were somewhat busy but unorganized. Mae was having a hard time with our accounting package so I couldn't get any financial information. I was in the dark. Clem and Luis were taking care of business that came over the phone, but they were idle most of the time. They were not the soliciting sales type like me. I sold a few homes for Tom but couldn't stand the pace. In pest control, I would sell fumigation or a pest control service nearly every day. Although the rewards were small the satisfaction of a sale was there on a renewing basis. In real estate the sales are infrequent. I was either up or down and not good for bipolar. I was very manic one afternoon and went into our office and gave Luis, Clem, and Mae a tongue lashing. Although Mae was working her hardest, I wasn't getting the numbers. Clem and Luis were not living up to my expectations. When I am manic, nobody can. I was upset and vocal. My manic gradually turned to depression and I quit Delmore Realty and started working full-time for Bowman Termite. I was there in body but not in mind because I couldn't concentrate, too much anxiety and I wasn't sleeping well. It got to the point where I couldn't go to work. The ups and downs were tearing me apart. Some people understand depression, especially those who have gone through it and some don't. Some think you can turn a switch on and off and it will go away.

There is no switch. If you are lucky, the right antidepressant may work, and if unlucky, it won't then on to another medications It may take more than a month to feel any results. There are many antidepressants and sometimes it may take a combination of two. There is no simple answer. I still walked in the morning with Tom, Young, and Evelyn, but I had very low energy and I could hardly say a word to Tom. I had a hard time completing my thoughts. He doesn't understand mental disorders. His sister was schizophrenic, until recently passing away. He always referred to her as his crazy sister, as helpless, and who couldn't take care of herself. He showed no empathy, although he may have been empathetic, he didn't show it. He helped her financially at times and did care about her, but it wasn't the same as empathy.

I gradually started walking in the mornings and afternoons because I was feeling a little better, but during the day I would lay in bed. For me the healing process is slow. Some people with bipolar have mood changes daily while my manic stage would last a couple of weeks, my depressed stage would last for several months. My sister Patty can remain depressed for a year or more at a time. The psychiatrists and I, didn't know I was bipolar. They were treating me for major depression because when I went to see them, I was depressed. My sister Pam, suggested to me that I may be bipolar. I had a hard time convincing my psychiatrist that I might be bipolar although I had all the symptoms.

The depression played its course at times I had suicidal thoughts. During a depression bout, you think it will never end. However, I was slowly able to get back some ability to concentrate and slowly the anxiety decreased. Sleeping would improve and I was finally able to get back to work. I would feel normal again, completing the full circle as I went back to setting goals for the company and then back to stress.

CHAPTER 24

The Last Semester of our Parent's Lives 1990–2004

Evelyn's father's health was on the decline. He had previously had quadruple bypass surgery for his weak heart and did very well after the surgery. In the early 1990s, he started suffering from dementia. At one point he was driving and got lost and couldn't get home. He was officially diagnosed as having Alzheimer's disease. As in the case of Alzheimer's his condition progressively got worse. Mommy did everything she could to take care of Daddy but she became overburdened. A family decision was made to bring Mommy and Daddy to Maui. Daddy was put in Hale Makua, a senior care home, for professional help and assistance and Mommy came to live with us. Evelyn and Ester were so good to their parents. They would take Mommy and visit Daddy, although he didn't know who they were. Daddy was still strong physically.

Mommy's health wasn't all that good. She had asthma, which was life-altering, and her eyes were always tearing due to an eye duct problem. Although the tearing was not life-altering, it was a nuisance. Mommy lived with Evelyn and me for six wonderful years and was and still is so special to me. I miss Mommy. Evelyn was a wonderful caregiver and Ester would come by frequently. Evelyn and her mother have a lot of characteristics in common. She passed away on August 1, 2002. Our family was saddened as the kids just adored her. Mommy was ninety years old when she passed. Daddy continued to live at Hale Makua waiting to join Mommy. He passed away on October 2, 2004, at the age of ninety-one.

My mother passed away in 1994. She was a very fit person. I thought she would live to be 100. We all thought she would outlive Dad but that wasn't the case. When Mom was about seventy-five years old, she was starting to have problems. She had some vision loss but more than anything, it was her jaw that was so painful. She went to her doctor, and he recommended for her to see a dentist. Her dentist informed her that her problem was not dental and recommended that she see a medical doctor. She did, but her doctor was confused with her diagnosis and initially diagnosed her wrong. I just googled Symptom: painful jaw and change in vision and I got Temporal Arteritis and that is what she had, but google was just in its infancy when Mom was diagnosed. With the onset of Temporal Arteritis early diagnosis is very important. Mom was losing her vision quickly, in fact, she went blind. She was a very determined person even as she aged; she learned braille. She would even handwrite letters and would not dwell on the negative.

After going blind, Mom kept their house in tip-top shape as she did before she became blind. According to sister Julie, she even washed windows although she couldn't see. Once her condition was diagnosed, she was put on heavy doses of steroids. Along with the steroids she got the side effects including weight gain and her face was swollen, she bruised easily, she had low muscle strength which affected her heart. She died from either too many steroids or Temporal Arteritis; we are not sure. She was an inspiration to us all. Mom and Dad were married for fifty-six years.

That was the saddest day for my dad. He lost his sweetheart, his companion, and his arguing buddy. They loved each other very much. Mom did everything for Dad as Evelyn has done for me. Dad was lost as I know I will be if Evelyn passes first. Dad was seventy-nine when Mom passed away. The next nine years were going to be tough and lonely. My sister Bonnie was so good with him and would give him a lot of attention. They would often go out to dinner or just talk. He missed Mom so much. Dad had friends in the neighborhood, and he would often go for a walk, but he was lonely. Pam would visit frequently, Patty not so often and Julie and I the least due to living out of state. When Julie lived in California she would often go fishing with Dad. As he aged, his memory was lapsing so it was decided that it was best to put him in a care home. Those last three years were tough. He never was a big eater and Evelyn and I saw him near the end of his life when he was so frail and thin. It is hard to get old. "I miss you, Mom and Dad."

CHAPTER 25

Building the Family Business with Family 2001–2021

On Oahu, Jill was making eyes at this good-looking baseball pitcher for the University of Hawaii, (UH). He had an unusual first name, Wakon. She wondered how he got that name because he looked like he was from Hawaii, but she had never heard the name Wakon before. She asked Jamie Aloy, her high school classmate and starting first baseman for UH to introduce her to Wakon. When they were introduced, Wakon said, "Howdy, Jill, my name is Wakon." It may not have been those exact words but once Wakon started talking, she knew he was not from Hawaii. Jill found out that he was from a little town near Tulsa, Oklahoma. Wakon was on a full scholarship to play baseball. Shortly after they were introduced. they started dating. Wakon is a good-looker and is mostly American Indian. His mother, Liz is 100% Creek Indian and his father, Tom is Creek and German. Wakon is about 5'9" and muscular.

Evelyn and I planned to go to see Wakon pitch and meet his parents, who were coming from Tulsa to watch Wakon play ball. Two days prior, in the early morning hours, Evelyn was woken by a loud scream. It was mine and I was bleeding profusely from my mouth, and I was seizing. I didn't feel anything because I was unconscious. The ambulance was called, and I recovered except for my tongue. I had almost bitten it off. When I met Liz and Tom I couldn't talk or eat. Tom is about 6'4" and burly and Liz is the same as Evelyn, 5'. They could pass for sisters; however, Evelyn is Filipino, and Liz is Creek Indian. I don't think I made a great impression on Wakon's parents.

As they got to know each other better, Jill inquired about Wakon's major. You know, the typical questions asked when getting acquainted. Wakon replied, sociology. She asked him what he wanted to do after college. He didn't have a clue; all he had ever done was play sports and video games. He said most athletes take majors like sociology. Sociology graduates solve social problems. Jill wondered what kind of problems Wakon was going to solve. She was in the Dental Hygiene program at UH and nearing completion. Upon completion, she could find a job paying $35/hour. That was good money in 2003. Wakon was a likely prospect as a professional baseball player but became unlikely when he realized he needed Tommy John surgery on his pitching arm. Jill was in the last year of her Dental Hygiene school and almost ready to make money and her boyfriend, Wakon was going to solve social problems. Wakon realized his first social problem was to find a way to make money. His UH degree wasn't going to cut the mustard. He decided to enroll at Seminole College in Oklahoma in a master's program for Educational Technology. Jill, still studying on Oahu, waited for Wakon to return.

Wakon returned sooner than expected. He missed Jill too much and decided to come back to Hawaii. He was able to get a scholarship at the University of Hawaii and continue his master's program. With his master's degree in hand, they were married on August 9, 2003. A beautiful wedding took place in our backyard. There were over 10,000 lights, well, maybe not quite 10,000 that lit up everything. The trees, shrubs, plants, statues, and gazebo were all brightly adorned. I know because I was taking them down for years afterward. Jill and Wakon were a very handsome couple. I had the privilege of walking Jill down to Wakon and the minister.

It wasn't long after their wedding that they moved from Oahu to Maui. Jill was able to get a job quickly and Wakon was interviewing. We thought he would work for a private school such as Kamehameha or Seabury, two of our best Maui private schools. While he was interviewing, he would help me, when he had time. We painted our house together. He was a hard worker and he learned quickly. He also helped me at the office to solve computer problems. He was great at computers, and I was weak. I was better at creating computer problems. He wasn't getting much feedback from his interviews and out of the clear blue sky, he said "Dad, I could work for you." I could use someone like Wakon, but I wouldn't be able to pay him that much. A person with a master's degree working for an upstart pest control company? I thought he could do better. On the other hand, I could use him so we hired Wakon on July 1, 2004. That was nearly eighteen years ago.

Bowman Termite was growing in size but not necessarily in profits. I was only able to give Wakon modest salary increases, which were much less than what he should have been paid. It wasn't too long after Wakon came on board we started to do our own tent fumigation. When we started Bowman, we decided not to do tent fumigation. I arranged with a local fumigator to sub-out our fumigations. After a few years of subbing our fumigations, we had a change of heart. We had enough fumigation coming in and with Wakon on board, we decided to do our own fumigations. We are currently the second-largest fumigator in the state. In the beginning, our fumigation crew on Maui wasn't very reliable. There was one time they cooked themselves breakfast at a customer's house, using the customer's food and utensils. Wakon fired that crew.

There was another time that our lead fumigator was asleep on the job having his crew do all the work. In Hilo, our fumigator was doing side jobs and a salesman was driving drunk at 10:00 am. Over time we got rid of the bad apples. Wakon was a tremendous help in the growth of the company. He took the initiative to look at and start new sources of business. Term-i-mesh, a stainless-steel mesh barrier used to prevent subterranean termites from entering structures, was being written into certain specifications for termite treatments. Wakon researched it thoroughly and was able to get licensed to use Term-i-Mesh. There are only a handful of companies licensed in Hawaii. He also researched bird netting. We have done $507,000 in new revenue for Term-i-Mesh and $234,000 in bird netting in the last three and a half years. He has looked into other areas, some have generated income, and some haven't. A good businessperson should look for opportunities to increase revenue when they are not manic.

About ten years after opening Bowman on Maui, we considered opening an office on the Big Island in Hilo. We wanted to have Clem be the branch manager, but he declined. We considered Ralph who was competent and had been with our company for several years. Ralph felt somewhat insecure and said he would go to Hilo if we hired a former coworker to work in the office. We interviewed and hired Gaye at Ralph's suggestion. She was trained in the Maui office, and once trained we felt we were ready to go to Hilo. Evelyn and I went over to rent a house and get situated. Home prices in Hilo were cheap compared to Maui so we didn't rent a house, we bought one. We brought Ralph, Alia, his wife, and their two children and Gaye over to `Hilo from Maui. We all lived together for several months getting the business off the ground floor. Evelyn and I would go back and forth in the beginning. Ralph and Gaye worked out of the house and Ralph stocked up his truck with chemicals and Gaye set up an office in the house. We decided it was time to look for office/warehouse space. Evelyn and I spoke to Rick Barbardi, a realtor. I told him about our office in Maui.

We had an older home in a commercial zone, which permitted our type of business. He said I may know of something. We saw it and the owner said he would sell it to us for $325,000, which was a lot more than it was worth. When you are manic that doesn't matter. We paid the price although the appraisal came in much lower. Behind the house was a structure that we could make into our office. It was unpermitted but who cares when you are manic. Evelyn and I moved into the house and contemplated the needs of the office. Too late, I was depressed. I couldn't contemplate. I couldn't think. Anxious thoughts were racing through my mind. I was so fortunate to have Wakon overseeing our Maui operations during my highs and lows.

Evelyn and I lived in Hilo for almost three years. While in Hilo, I went through depression often with some bouts were worse than others. Evelyn was there for support, driving me to some of my appointments and being by my side, but I needed more than that. My psychiatrist in Hilo seemed confused; the medicine wasn't working.

This was the psychiatrist whom I told I may be bipolar. He thought I was crazy, maybe I was, but he didn't think I was bipolar. He reluctantly admitted later that I was bipolar, but still never prescribed the proper medication. I love Hilo, I love the people and our Hilo employees, but I had many tough times. Our operations there has done quite well, looking back eleven years later, we couldn't be prouder, but it was tough for me.

My last major bout of depression was about two years after Evelyn and I returned from Hilo to Maui. Jill and Wakon had put an offer on a two-story house that was going through a bank sale. Jill, Wakon, and the kids, Aidan and Ayana, moved into our house. I was starting to feel anxiety before they moved in. Scott, our lead fumigator, was driving our fumigation truck without a CDL license. He got a ticket and he had to go to court along with me. I was sure I was going to jail.

This incident triggered anxiety and depression. This depression bout was a bad one as I wasn't able to go to work for quite a while. Jill was very concerned. I was going to a psychiatrist upcountry who tried many medications that weren't working. The last one he recommended was Wellbutrin. This antidepressant is not supposed to be used if you are on antiseizure medication, which I was.

When I mentioned I was on antiseizure medication, he advised me to take it anyway. I give up.... For the last several years I had taken so many different antidepressants and nothing appeared to be helping. He mentioned that I was a likely candidate for shock treatment. I was willing to try almost anything. Fortunately, Ester, Evelyn's sister, said, "Why don't you see Dr. Arensdorf?" He was a child psychiatrist, and we knew the family. When I saw him, I provided some of my medical histories. He asked if I had ever tried Lithium. Lithium is a chemical on our periodic chart and is used in batteries. Do I need a new battery? I have tried almost everything else and it might be better than shock treatment. I said "No, but I have tried Eveready batteries." No, I did not say that; I was not in the mood.

When I am depressed, I have no sense of humor. I did say, no, I have never tried Lithium. I asked him, "How does Lithium work? He explained that it is a mood stabilizer. Being bipolar, this is a highly recommended treatment. He had me try Lithium in combination with Quetiapine (Seroquel). Quetiapine is classified as an atypical antipsychotic used for the treatment of schizophrenia, bipolar disorder, and major depressive disorder. It is not an SSRI like the antidepressants that I had previously taken. I took several SSRIs, including Celexa, Lexapro, Prozac, Paxil, and Zoloft. I also took Cymbalta, an SNRI, and Wellbutrin belonging to the NDRI class.

Nine years have passed since my last episode of depression. Lithium in combination with Seroquel worked for me. This has been the biggest relief in my life. But why didn't the other psychiatrist prescribe Lithium and Seroquel? According to *Psychiatric Times*, May 13, 2020 Lithium and Seroquel are the top two drugs recommended for bipolar disorder. My depression lasted around twenty-five years. Why did it take so long for a proper diagnosis? Once I was diagnosed, why did it take so long to get the right medication? Most of the time I was functional but much of the time I wasn't. The swings of going in and out of depression took a toll. During my depression, were the associated anxiety, a lot of sleepless nights, a lethargic feeling, a lack of sense of worth, and a loss of my sense of humor. Some say they may feel sad. I don't think that is the appropriate term for the way I felt. I wasn't happy but I felt overwhelmed and confused with racing thoughts going through my head, but sad isn't the right word for me.

Understanding depression is very difficult for those who have never had depression. Why are there so many suicides? One of the main reasons for suicide is depression and according to Mental Health America, 30–70% of suicide victims suffer from major depression or bipolar disorder. Depression plays a role in more than one-half of suicide attempts in the US, and suicide is the tenth leading cause of death in the US. Evelyn and I are aware of seven people who have committed suicide. Five were here on Maui. An apparent successful minister and his wife took their lives. They lived in our subdivision in Waiehu Heights and had just built a large, beautiful church. A college student from Maui took his life. I spoke to his father before the suicide. His father told me that his son had attempted to take his life.

I told the father about my depression and that he should take his son to a psychiatrist as soon as possible. I don't know if he did. His son committed suicide less than a month after our discussion. Jennifer's sister-in-law lost her husband to suicide. He left his wife and their three kids behind. Within the last year, we lost a bright, energetic, likable employee to suicide due to depression. My brother-in-law, married to my sister Patty, ended his life by suicide and our relative from the San Francisco Bay area took her life. She was here on Maui less than two weeks prior. She was sixteen years old. She appeared normal, happy, and content as she hung out with her cousins.

In 2013, I discussed with Evelyn thoughts about the transfer of the company. Evelyn and I were getting on in age. At that time Wakon was the only family member working for the company and he was a very big part of its success. I called him into my office to have an open discussion regarding the future of the company regarding ownership. He shied away and our discussion was shallow. He wasn't ready to discuss the matter. To this date, I am not sure why he was so reserved. I waited about a year, and we met again, this time with our accountant and Evelyn. He still wasn't ready. It seemed as if something was bothering him. He was quite moody for a long time. I eventually drew up a plan of ownership that involved our three kids. Jeff had indicated a desire to come back to Maui. I told him that I wanted him to work in the company with Wakon. Jill showed an interest in working for the company. I planned to turn the business to the kids. They would be great assets—51% of the business would go to Jill and 24½ % would go to Jennifer and Jeff. Jennifer and Jeff would own the office, which was a nice piece of real estate. I wanted to be as fair as possible. We had meetings on our lanai and discussed the ramifications of business ownership. I stressed that they should be open with each other and gave them examples of family company failures on Maui that ended in the family separating and not trusting one another.

We all had tears in our eyes because that is the last thing we wanted. I emphasized that a business takes a lot of work, and it has its rewards and drawbacks. We agreed to a three-year plan. After the first year, they would own 1/3, second-year 2/3, and after the third year, they would have complete ownership. In 2018, Bowman Termite did $5,529,800 in revenue and we had approximately 40 employees. We had gotten rid of the bad apples and were surrounded by some tremendous, dedicated, honest employees. Many had been with us for a long time. To mention a few, Clem and I have worked together for 43 years, Mae and Sande for close to 25 years, Ralph 19 years, Wakon 17 years, Scott 15 years, Jay, 14 years, Leka, Makai, and Len, three brothers over 13 years, Shelli, 12 years, Big Jeff 12 years, Michael 12 years, Alvin, 12 years, Darrell,12 years. We emphasize training, fairness, and honesty and it has worked.

Shelli and her husband Gordon have been such a big attribute to the company. Shelli is our service manager and is the administrator and commander in chief of the pest control department. Gordon sees that everything gets done. They are a great team. The three years went without a glitch. Jill and Jeff became full-time employees. Jill is the back-office manager doing the majority of accounting and payroll and in charge of Wakon. (Not really) Wakon took full charge and has managed the company successfully and profitably since the transfer. Jeff became his right-hand person learning the business quickly. I taught classes to both Jill and Jeff to prepare them for licensing and then I spent a couple of months in the field with Jeff. Jeff also learned a lot from Wakon. Within two years Bowman Termite had grown another 20% and our staff grew to fifty employees.

Jeff and Jill are both doing great in their jobs, and they are very good with the employees and most importantly, they enjoy it. Jennifer is employed as a nurse at the hospital and may eventually work with Bowman in the future if she desires. Evelyn works in the office with Jill and is not ready to retire. For the last six months, I have been working four days a week, but beginning this week I will be working three days per week. I hardly spend any time in the office. I primarily do outside sales and inspections. I don't make any business decisions because I am never asked to. I enjoy the lack of stress and thoroughly enjoy the fact that the business is run by the family.

CHAPTER 26

Trips were a Big Part of our Lives

When our granddaughter, Tiare was just two years old we went on an Alaskan cruise and a bus tour of the Canadian Rockies. We sold Maui Fumigation and decided to take a super vacation. It was. The cruise was fabulous as the kids got to eat as much as they wanted and what they wanted. Jennifer chose to eat carrots. She had an orange glow about her and was borderline anorexic. It didn't last long, but she had us concerned. The kids, Jennifer, Jill, Jeff, including Tiare were excellent travelers and on the cruise, there was so much for the kids to do. Going to Glacier Bay was a real highlight. After debarking from the cruise, we boarded a bus to discover the Canadian Rockies. That was our first bus tour, and our tour guide was phenomenal. Evelyn and I loved the bus tour way of traveling as it was relaxing, and the tour guide did all the work. We went on many bus tours after this and enjoyed each one.

We returned to the Philippines on two additional trips with Mommy. On our second trip, my most vivid memory is from the results of the three of us eating raw oysters. The "kasilyas" (toilets) were not close enough and because of the delicious oysters we did not fare too well for a few days. On our last trip, we went to attend Uncle Jose's funeral. Uncle Jose was Mommy's closest brother and his funeral was a big ordeal. This was in Dingras and it appeared as if the whole town was there. The service was at a small church, very solemn on the inside and outside was festive as many of the attendees were inebriated from their homemade wine and spirits. Some of the ladies and farmworkers were chewing betel nut with their red-stained teeth. People chew it for its nicotine-like effects from this strong stimulant. Several ladies were squatting and smoking their rolled tobacco as they do it a little differently, the lit end is inside the mouth. Mommy used to smoke this way in Honolulu. After the funeral, Uncle Jose's casket was taken from the church, and it journeyed from village to village on its route to Baguio and at each stop, friends and relatives would mourn his death.

When going from town to town in the Philippines the first thing you notice is the beautifully adorned churches. There is a lot of money spent to build them and keep them beautiful, then you notice all the small and usually run-down houses. I wonder where all their money went?

After Baguio, on our last Philippine trip, we took a special excursion to the Banaue Rice Terraces. From Baguio to Banaue it is only 114 miles by bus but it takes nearly nine hours to get there. That is 12.666667 miles per hour and I am not exaggerating or underestimating. Evelyn, her mom, and I boarded a common fare bus and journeyed the steep, windy, and narrow road. Everything and anything would be loaded on the bus including a rack on top to carry bicycles, animals in cages, and other miscellaneous cargo. The inside of the bus was cramped but thank God we weren't in Manila where it would be hot and muggy. It wasn't hot as the temperature was in the 60's. We started at an elevation of 4,600 feet in Baguio and ended in Banaue with a similar elevation depending on what part of Banaue.

Just before arriving in Banaue, we saw beautiful, terraced mountains planted with rice. The Igorots are the indigenous people of the Philippines with an estimated population was approximately 1,500,000 in the early twenty-first century. They primarily inhabit the mountains in northern Luzon and were notorious headhunters before the twentieth century. The rice terraces were formed and maintained by these indigenous people over 2,000 years ago until the present, according to some historians. They were formed with basic tools and by hand, an engineering feat of tremendous magnitude. It has been called the "Eighth wonder of the world." The gravity flow irrigation system allowed the rice to flourish.

Another early vacation was to New Zealand. Our neighbor did home swaps and we met this wonderful older couple who stayed in their home and were from New Zealand. We became friends and they invited us to visit them at their home in Nelson in the northern part of the South Island. We took them up on their offer. New Zealand is beautiful and there is such a variety of scenic landscapes with the grass so green, and the sheep are so plentiful. We took pictures at the gorge where they invented bungee jumping and we took a helicopter ride over the glaciers, and stopped at a botanical garden where Evelyn got pooped on. As we entered this botanical garden, I looked up and saw a large bird about the size of a goose fly over. It let loose right over my head, but I ducked (pun not intended) and "pooped on Evelyn's head." What a mess. Evelyn rarely has one hair out of place and now she has been pooped on. Fortunately for me, and maybe for her, there were two young Japanese girl tourists quick to her assistance. They had Evelyn cleaned up as I was taking pictures of the three of them.

One very special bus tour was to Copper Canyon. My former neighbor on Oahu ran a bus tour out of Phoenix, Arizona and he told me about the Copper Canyon tour as being his favorite. Evelyn and I investigated it and decided to go. Great decision! We left Phoenix and took a bus tour into the Sierra Madre Mountains in Mexico. Eventually, we boarded a train for the last hour segment. The tour is very scenic and breathtaking, seeing the canyons that were gorged by water millions of years ago. About an hour before our arrival to the top where our accommodations are located, it started snowing. It was beautiful. When there, we learned of the culture of the Tarahumara's, the indigenous people from that area. When the Spanish invaded Mexico, the Tarahumara people went deeper and deeper into the canyons to avoid the Spanish. There are estimated to be between 35,000 to 70,000 Tarahumaras. This is similar to the situation with the Igorots of Banaue, Philippines. The Tarahumara have adapted to life by running long distances. Overall, they are very shy people, and because of their nature, there is opposition regarding over-tourism in the area. This trip was very educational, and our group was a joy to be with.

There were a few years that we put Europe on our itinerary. Sisters Julie and Pam, Evelyn and I went to Portugal together. When I was growing up, Julie and I didn't know each other very well because she is six years older and me being a brat, wasn't a good combination and I didn't like her pinching. In traveling together, we learned that we loved each other. Pam and Julie are so much fun to be with on trips, with Julie being smart and organized and one who pays attention to instructions and details and Pam doesn't. Pam is just fun to be with. In addition to Portugal, we went to Russia. That is one of my very favorite trips. It was a river cruise on the Volga River. We started in St. Petersburg and ended in Moscow. It was so relaxing and educational. We asked Julie and Pam if they would like to join us on a return trip to Copper Canyon. They did, and we all enjoyed it.

When our kids were starting to have their kids, we went to New York all together as a big family and to Orlando, Florida to Disney World. The whole family went together and then to sister Julie's house in Sequim, Washington. One of the highlights of that trip was our visit to the retired animal zoo where you get to see all the animals taking naps.

We also traveled with Greg, Evelyn's brother, and his wife Sue. We went to Japan and Italy and the Netherlands and had great times. Two of our favorite trips we took on our own were to Thailand and Vietnam. In Thailand, we had the most wonderful time because our tour group mixed so well. We became close friends with Victor and Christina, a couple from southern California. We have seen them on many occasions since Thailand and we went to Ecuador with them where Christina was born. Victor is from Mexico, that is where we are going next. They are a young couple, younger than our kids and they had their first child last year. Evelyn and I seem to gravitate to young people or they to us, I'm not sure.

We went on a few big cruise ships but found those not to be our preferred choice of travel. We went through the Panama Canal on one cruise when we traveled with Monette and her husband, Paul, Paul's cousin, Len and his wife, Sylvia, three of his best friends from grade school, Jeff, Ken, and Ken and their wives, Linda, Nancy, and Rachael, all joined us. We had a big and fun group; the only problem was I started feeling anxiety come on. I wasn't myself, the "happy-go-lucky Bruce." I was the anxious, no confident, paranoid Bruce. I avoided conversation and I avoided our group as much as I could. On one of the last days when we were out to sea, I isolated myself by walking around the ship all day. I logged over fifteen miles that day. It was boring, and I was sore the next week, but I didn't have to talk to anyone.

There was one other trip I went on when I was depressed. My granddaughter Tiare got accepted into Brown University and we went to her indoctrination. Evelyn, Jennifer, and Jill were going, and I was going to stay home alone. The thought of that even got me more depressed so I told Evelyn that I wanted to go even though I wasn't in my right frame of mind. She agreed, so depressed Bruce went to Rhode Island, the home of Brown. It was probably the best that I did go, however, even with the love of Evelyn and the support of my beautiful daughters, suicide was on my mind but I survived to write about it.

Another cruise worth mentioning was our Elvis Cruise. Jimmy, Monette's brother is an Elvis impersonator. He is Filipino, about 5'4", and weighs close to 180. He can sing, his Elvis impersonation is fantastic but who cares if you can detect a slight Filipino accent? Beverly, Jimmy's wife, Paul, and Monette joined us on that cruise. We departed out of Mobile, Alabama. I never saw so many people proceeding to board the ship, exceeding their body mass index. We had so much fun, and Jimmy was great, Beverly super, Monette entertaining and, Paul somewhat tolerable. No, he is always a lot of fun, but don't let him know I said that.

We truly enjoyed every bus tour we went on. China, Spain, the Czech Republic, Netherlands, Nova Scotia, Montreal, and Toronto were all super trips. We have been to Australia two times and Ireland. For the past several years we were taking on average two trips per year. In February 2019, we had tickets to tour Mexico City and then into the Yucatan Peninsula. COVID-19 was starting to act up and we were concerned about catching Covid in Mexico. We canceled the trip and instead went to visit sister Pam in California and got to see Bonnie for a short time, but Patty wasn't up to it. Then we took a train ride to Monterey, California, and stopped in San Luis Obispo to see Cal Poly, where Teva, my grandson, is attending. I graduated from Cal Poly, Pomona, a sister campus way back in 1971.

Teva is a sophomore and couldn't attend classes due to COVID for his freshman year as all of his classes were online. We visited the campus and saw some students, but it was rather sparse. From there we were able to get back on the train and go to Monterey where we caught an Uber and went to Carmel to visit my favorite cousin, Delia. Delia was our tour guide and on the second day, we got word that California was shutting down due to COVID-19. We called Hawaiian Airlines and couldn't get through so we went to the airport and there was nothing but confusion. Our flight was canceled. We had no idea what was going to happen and neither did anyone else. The next day the air cleared, and we were able to get a flight and return to Maui. We hope we can resume traveling soon. Traveling is very therapeutic for both Evelyn and me. Because of COVID-19, we have only taken one trip in the past two years. Jill, Jennifer, Evelyn, and I, accompanied Teva to Cal Poly. Boy, is he ever spoiled. My mother never visited me in college, and it was only thirty miles away. Teva gets his aunty, mom, and grandparents from Hawaii to visit California to make sure he is okay. It was different in my days, my parents didn't come to my wedding.

CHAPTER 27

This is Not the Last Chapter

My epilepsy is hard to analyze. In review, my memory loss was the reason for my antiseizure medication. I did not have any seizures that I was aware of, although the amnesia may have been a form of a very rare seizure, Transient Epileptic Amnesia (TEA). After taking anti-seizure medication I had seizures including focal and grand-mal. The only grand-mal seizures I had were a result of skipping the medication. In my lifetime I have had three grand mal seizures and roughly fifty focal seizures. With a grand mal seizure, you lose consciousness, and you have violent muscle contractions. Grand mal seizures are located on both sides of the brain. In focal seizures, the brain is affected on one side. With my focal aware seizures, I would experience an "aura," in which I would have an unusual smell or a good feeling like déjà vu. This feeling is hard to explain. and it would only last for a few seconds. That was it for me. Some may experience different symptoms such as muscle jerking or stiffening, a sudden sense of fear, depression or happiness, or a change in heart rate, breathing, sweating, or goose bumps. These seizures last for a very short time and there is no loss of consciousness.

After my third grand mal seizure, Evelyn took over managing my medications and has enforced them rigorously. Since I have been consistent with the medications for epilepsy, I haven't had a seizure for over eighteen years. As far as memory, I can't remember what I don't remember, so it must be good. Seriously, I think my memory now is quite normal. Since everything has gone well for the last eighteen years, I decided to talk to my Neurologist to see if I could get off my medication. Dilantin can cause damage to the liver, so if you don't need it, why take it? I set up a doctor's appointment recently. I have only seen this Neurologist on one other occasion about ten years ago, for the same reason. She had me answer a questionnaire with about ten questions that she entered into the computer. The information coming back indicated that I have a 34% chance of having a seizure if I discontinued my medications. That made my choice easy; it was a no-brainer; I chose to continue my medication. What the computer can do with algorithms is amazing.

Being forty years old when I suffered my first Bipolar episode, I was a late bloomer because bipolar disorders generally start when a person is in their mid-twenties and is generally equal for men and women. I had experienced episodes of bipolar depression for over twenty-five years until I was finally prescribed the right medication. I wonder what my life would have been like if I were correctly diagnosed initially and put on Lithium and Seroquel much earlier? For that twenty-five years, I was put on several antidepressants, but they weren't addressing my problem. Lithium is a mood stabilizer, and that was my missing link to being well. In retrospect, I am disappointed and bewildered. The episodes were occurring more frequently. I was finally diagnosed as being bipolar after twenty-two years. My diagnosis for the twenty-two years was major depression, not bipolar. but for three years after my bipolar diagnosis, I was still not prescribed the proper medication. I was only prescribed anti-depressants.

A proper diagnosis was given only after my sister Pam suggested that I tell my psychiatrist that I may be bipolar. There is bipolar I and bipolar II. I am bipolar II. People with bipolar I have greater manic episodes and generally can't function at work during the manic stage. I was hypomanic, not manic. Generally, my manic episodes would be associated with a new project, such as starting a new aspect of our business-like bringing TADD Dogs to Hawaii, opening Water Gardens of Hawaii, JewelWay, opening Bowman Termite, or opening our Hilo Branch on the Big Island. These five events, along with more, were affected because of my bipolar disorder, some good and some bad. I would get an idea and would become so focused. Things wouldn't get in my way, sometimes even reasoning. During my mania, I required less sleep and was sometimes unstoppable. Even after my condition was diagnosed as bipolar II, my psychiatrist continued to prescribe only antidepressants to no avail. Moving back to Maui, I sought out a new Psychiatrist. I provided the information from my Hilo Psychiatrist regarding my diagnosis.

My Maui psychiatrist took the same route, more antidepressants, and no mood stabilizers, and the same results, bipolar depression. That is when he recommended that I look into "shock therapy." I considered it because I was feeling desperate. This was after about twelve monthly sessions with him. I was grabbing straws. That is when my sister-in-law suggested I visit another psychiatrist, one that my nephew had been to. I visited my last psychiatrist who recommended Lithium and Seroquel right off the bat. Within weeks I became stable, and my bipolar condition was managed. It has been nearly ten years that I have been free of bipolar symptoms.

Is my bipolar condition a result of genetics? I don't know, but according to research it most likely is. Two of my grandparents suffered from depression to the best of my knowledge. In their time, depression was much less understood and rarely discussed. They were never diagnosed because they never went to the doctors and Paxil and Prozac were not yet available. In the very early days, depression was thought to be spiritual, caused by demons and the anger of the gods. It was dealt with by priests rather than physicians. However, there were those doctors that believed depression was biological. Around 25 BCE, harsh treatments of starvation and beatings were given to the mentally ill. Along with Christianity in the Middle Ages, depression was associated with the devil, demons, or witches. Exorcisms, drowning, and burning were popular treatments. Many people were locked up in so-called "lunatic-asylums."

In the eighteenth and nineteenth centuries, depression became viewed as a weakness in temperament that was inherited and could not be changed. Some doctors prescribed water immersion for as long as possible without drowning and using spinning stools to put the brains back in their correct position. Sometimes vomiting was prescribed. In 1917 Sigmund Freud used psychoanalysis or talk therapy to reduce self-destructive thoughts and behaviors. It wasn't until the 1950s that drugs were introduced into the treatment of depression. Some of the first antidepressants to be used were Tofranil and other tricyclic antidepressants. (TCAs). However, there were serious side effects associated with (TCAs).

Prozac was first marketed in 1987, Zoloft in 1991, and Paxil in 1992. These (SSRI's) selective serotonin reuptake inhibitors, target serotonin levels in the brain and usually have fewer side effects. Some additional non-medical treatments included exercise, music, diet, and talking to your friends and a doctor, but these alone will not generally manage the problem. A combination of antidepressants and mood stabilizers is essential for bipolar management. (Much of the information regarding depression was obtained from https://www.verymind.com)

What triggered my bipolar episodes? I feel my manic stage was generally started by some type of business plan. When manic, I would get carried away with grandiose thoughts of higher than realistic business aspirations. These thoughts would take over, and my logic would suffer as well as reality. Then I would come to a realization stage. "Oops, my plan is not working" and then I would decline to the depression stage. According to the common list of bipolar triggers for depression, mine was most likely caused by stress, lack of sleep, and anxiety. The Dilantin that I take as an antiseizure medication appears unlikely to be a trigger.

I am a high-energy person; I am competitive, and I have a lot of drive even without mania. With mania, watch out. If I am in a conversation, I feel I know what the person is going to say so I interrupt with MY MORE IMPORTANT THOUGHTS. I have a feeling of grandeur, thinking I am invincible. I have a feeling of being obsessed with and completely absorbed in an activity I am focused on; I am extremely confident, which opens me up to impulsive behavior. Mania is a great feeling. You feel invincible. When you are manic you feel your IQ has raised to a new level. I remember one morning on a walk with Tom, I was feeling manic. I proceeded to raise my arms in the air and yell "I AM MANIC," then I ran up this steep hill as if I were Usain Bolt. Tom thought I was crazy, rightfully so. In my manic stage, although I wasn't always in touch with reality, I didn't do anything to physically harm myself or anyone else. I was recently talking to a person about bipolar disorders. He mentioned that one of his female associates refused to take medicine because she didn't want to disrupt her manic stages. I am not sure if he was making up a story or what. To me, depression is not worth mania and irrational thinking is certainly not good for business.

My manic stages were almost always followed by depression. Manic was mostly fun, depression was no fun. My depression feelings were almost the opposite of my manic feelings. They would come on gradually. I would start to lose my confidence, my ability to concentrate, my sense of humor, and my drive. I recall one episode of depression as I was doing estimating for Bowman Termite, my company. I realized I was going into depression. I was losing my ability to concentrate. I would measure a house to determine the cubic measurement to price for fumigation, a task that I had done for over thirty years. I had problems. I couldn't concentrate. However, after a concerted struggle, I finally managed.

Toward the end of the week, I couldn't even measure houses. I would go back to my office and just sit until the end of the workday. On Friday of that week, I went to prepare a customer for fumigation and couldn't do it. My speech was garbled, and I couldn't concentrate. I was no longer able to work. I had very low energy, and a lack of motivation, food didn't appeal to me, and I felt worthless. I did not want to go into the office and see our wonderful staff. It was my birthday, of all days, and I did go back. My office was all decorated with birthday balloons, streamers, glitter, and the like. It was decorated by my secretaries. They wanted to make me feel better. It made me feel worse. I wanted to hide. I just wanted to go home, which I did. I didn't come back for several months. My depression got much worse before it got better. I had thoughts of suicide, but I had Evelyn's support and love. When depressed your mind is filled with negative thoughts and you think the depression is going to last forever, but there is usually light at the end of the tunnel, but you can't see it. My most severe depression bout lasted approximately three months. When depressed, time goes by so slowly. I am an optimist when not depressed, so I can look on the bright side. I always lost weight, and, in my case, my depression was followed by normalcy for longer times than my depression. After an episode of depression, one appreciates normalcy. I didn't have to sit on a stool and spin to get my brains back in order. Today's medications are better, science is better, and information is so much more readily available on the internet. A proper Psychiatrist, capable of providing an accurate diagnosis is so vitally important in bipolar treatment.

There are good ones out there. There is good information on the internet. word of caution, only read it when you are not having a bipolar episode. If you get depressed or you know someone who is depressed, get help. Don't give up. If someone is depressed, show empathy. Depressed people don't fake depression. They are ill. Many people who have or had bipolar are household names and have become very successful. Some included are, Ernest Hemingway, Ted Turner, Vivian Leigh, Frank Sinatra, Jane Pauley, Patty Duke, Mariah Carey, Mel Gibson, Kurt Cobain, Winston Churchill, Britney Spears, and Bruce Bowman.

I am now seventy-three but have been depression-free for ten years. It not only caused hardships for me but my family and business. Things could have been a lot worse. Evelyn was so supportive, and the kids took it in stride. We were very fortunate to have tremendous employees who pulled even harder when I was down. Although there is no cure, I am on proper medication and doing fine. I am looking forward to a lot more travels with Evelyn and my sisters and friends, watching my grandkids grow up and getting married in our backyard, and seeing Wakon, Jill, and Jeff and their wonderful staff succeed in the business and so many more things.

In conclusion, I have worked hard, but life has been good to me. I do have a sincere concern for the mentally ill. Mental illnesses are often so misunderstood. Being mentally ill myself, I realize how it can be very difficult to cope with the realities of life. I was extremely fortunate to have Evelyn, my wife of forty-eight years. She cared for me and loved me through each episode. She prepares my medication every day and scolds me if I am an hour late in taking it. A lot of mentally ill do not have an Evelyn. Without care and empathy, they may end up on the street and become homeless and confused. Without Evelyn, I could have been there. There is help for the mentally ill, but it is underfunded.

Last month, I visited my Family Doctor to inquire about seeing another psychiatrist since mine recently retired. I haven't visited a psychiatrist for roughly two years. He told me that my medical insurance does not cover psychiatric visits anymore. He has been instructed by our insurance carrier to direct his patients to Betterhelp, an online therapy service. Its service is worldwide. This is a big cost saving for the insurance companies. I hope it works for the patients, however not having direct contact with a psychiatrist may be very hard for some mentally ill to cope with.

Proceeds from this book will be donated for support of the mentally ill.

Thank you and Mahalo

Bruce and Evelyn Bowman

APPENDIX

My Kids, Grandchildren, and Wife 1974–Present

Jennifer, our first daughter, was born on February 29, 1976. She is married to Kauila Pimental and they have four children. They have been married for twenty-two years. They were married in our backyard as all our kids were. Kauila and Jen went to Saint Anthony High School together and fell in love. Kauila generally has at least one and sometimes two jobs at a time. He works for the Andaz Hotel in banquet planning. Jen is a real beauty and is a registered nurse at Maui Memorial Hospital. She works with patients after they have had surgery. She is very caring, and her patients love her and so do the doctors and her coworkers. Jen is very efficient and fast at what she does including painting, cooking, house cleaning, you name it and if she can do it, it will be done fast. She is also very physically fit having run a couple of marathons and is very active in CrossFit. Her four kids, Tiare, Taysia, Teva, and Lilikoi are extremely lucky to have Jen as their "super mom." Jenifer was fifteen when she gave birth to Tiare. Evelyn was a big help in sharing the duties of raising Tiare when she was young, but Jennifer exceeded our expectations in motherhood. Fortunately, Tiare was an easy child to raise and Jen had plenty of help with Tiare's upbringing with love given by Jeff and Jill and Evelyn and me. She is also a mother to Taysia, Teva, and Lilikoi.

Tiare

Tiare was born on March 31, 1991. By then, Jen decided that Gary, Tiare's father, was not the right match for her. Evelyn and I were so relieved. She was also showing more respect for Evelyn and me. We were all together again living in our home. When Tiare was just two, we took an Alaskan cruise and did a bus tour of the Canadian Rockies. She was so well behaved, and we all had so much fun. We were paying for preschool, but it was more like a babysitting school. It wasn't Hongwanji. Evelyn withdrew her realizing she could do a better job, then to Waihee Elementary and Iao Intermediate School as her mom, and Jeff and Jill had done. She whizzed through school, but she had a girl classmate bully her at Iao. That was a tough time for her. She graduated from Baldwin High; the same school Jill went to. Jill graduated with honors; Tiare graduated top of her class as Valedictorian. We were all so proud to hear her speech. Tiare is very good at art and dance, and I think she could be good at almost anything she tried. Tiare is gifted with determination.

She was looking at colleges when she was in 8th grade. When we were in San Francisco she wanted to see Stanford University. She set her goals high. She ended up going to Brown University, which is a renowned Ivy League University. This was Jennifer's firstborn who was nearly aborted. We all thank our blessings that didn't happen. Tiare went on to get her MD from Tufts University in Boston. Three years ago, she married Michael Spector whom our family adores. They got married in our backyard and we had a wonderful gathering of his family and friends from the East Coast and ours from the West Coast and Hawaii. There were probably close to 150 attendees. Michael is also a graduate of Brown with a degree in computer science engineering. Since his graduation, he has worked in the field of artificial intelligence (AI). You would think he was a local boy if he had a tan and didn't talk. He is from Boston and is Caucasian and Chinese. Tiare, as of this writing, is in her third year of residency and we recently heard that she was awarded a plastic surgery fellowship. We wish she could speed it up before our wrinkles become permanent. Tiare is approaching thirty-one and looks maybe twenty-one. She is just over 5' tall, petite and pretty. Her patients can't believe she is their doctor. They are lucky she is.

Taysia

Taysia was born in Maui on January 24, 2000. She is nearly nine years younger than Tiare. Taysia went to Iao Preschool and the same elementary and intermediate school as Tiare. Taysia was different from Tiare from the start. Tiare was delicate but determined and Taysia was tomboyish and determined. In preschool, she was usually dirty and yet very cute. She was involved in sports, and she could be rough and tough. She played soccer and excelled in canoe paddling.

Her grades were good but not great. She had a lot of nervous energy. Where Tiare could sit and enjoy a book, Taysia was constantly on the move. She was always playing jokes on me. Although very active she was chubby and had a funny figure. Her bikini looked as if was ready to fall off while playing in the surf.

In about 8th grade she started growing. One of her favorite things to do was to come and stand butt to butt to me and say, "who's taller?" I was probably five inches taller, but she would do that again and again. Soon I was only three inches taller, then two inches taller. Now I am two inches shorter. She is 5'9" and I am 5'7" on a good morning. Taysia got accepted at Seabury Hall, a top private school in the state of Hawaii. Seabury is expensive and she got a full ride as an athlete canoe paddler and because she has some Hawaiian blood from Kauila's side. After Taysia graduated, she got recruited by San Diego State University to row. She finished her first year and decided to take some time off. The rowing wasn't the same as the canoeing was in Hawaii. She went back after a break and now is attending full-time. She is studying to become a physical therapist. Taysia decided to discontinue rowing. She is happier now living near San Diego State in a house occupied by eight other Hawaii students.

Teva

Teva is now twenty and was born on September 19, 2001. He was a welcome addition to Jennifer and Kauila because he was a boy. He was cute and energetic and was a good kid growing up. He loved his sports and was and still is a very good athlete. One thing he enjoyed more than anything was hanging out with Kauila. They would go fishing and hiking and spend a lot of time together. Kauila also coached Teva in many sports, especially soccer. Teva is a smart athlete, understanding the rules and then becoming a real team leader in every sport he plays. Teva is very competitive as are his sisters. He wrestled when he was about eleven years old and never lost a match.

His best game was soccer and football where he excelled. I think he started around seven years old and continued to play through high school. In his junior and senior years, he made the all-league selection. Teva was always modest about his achievements. He graduated in 2020 from Kamehameha High School with honors as a student and an athlete. He did not have a graduation ceremony due to

COVID. Jennifer planned his surprise graduation party. Under Covid restrictions, parties weren't permitted so she planned a drive around. There must have been 300 people to wish Teva success. They were instructed to drive past Teva's aunty Brandy's, house, as Teva would stand out and wave. Many people brought Hawaiian leis and envelopes of money to congratulate him. This is the custom in Hawaii, however most times you would get a hug and kiss but not during Covid. Teva was planning for college. I wanted him to go to Cal Poly, San Luis Obispo. He was thinking of a career in Civil Engineering. Cal Poly had a great reputation. He looked at some other schools, but his final choice was Cal Poly. This university is hard to get into with an acceptance rate of only 24%. and is ranked second to Stanford in engineering in California. Teva has spent his first year at Cal Poly never seeing the campus. All his studies were online. He has done well; all As and Bs. He started officially attending class in September of 2021. Jill, Jennifer, Evelyn, and I, tagged along with him to make sure he is on the right path. Jen keeps in touch almost daily. Her question to him is "Do you miss us?" To her disappointment, he says, "No." He loves it. He got involved on a coed soccer team and is playing flag football and studying. The first thing Evelyn asked is, "Do you miss my cooking?" He doesn't have to answer that, I know he does.

Lilikoi

Lilikoi is Kauila and Jennifer's adopted daughter. Lilikoi was officially adopted on November 9, 2021. Lilikoi was brought into this world by a troubled mother. Her mother had drugs and various problems with the police. Lilikoi, whom we call Lili, has two other sisters, Honeydew and Pumpkin, and possibly other siblings whom we haven't met. Lili is now nine years old, and I consider her one of the luckiest people alive. She went from a mother having addiction problems to Jennifer who had her feet solidly grounded. Jennifer had her problems at fourteen and overcame them. Lili's mother, as of today, still has major problems. She is currently on probation and fled the country. She was the driver of a vehicle involved in a burglary. It was fortunate Jen and Kauila were willing to help Lili at the time they did. She was two years old. It has been over six years of Lili being with them and finally, the adoption is now history. It wasn't easy but both have big hearts. Lili was a fussy eater and still is. Jen and Lili got so close to each other and Lili, being a bright girl, was quick to learn. Lili has a super memory, and she is very logical. We think she could develop to become a great lawyer. Harvard, here she comes. We like to plant the seed early for our grandkids. After she earns her law degree, she plans to work in adoption services to speed up the process.

Jill, Wakon, and Children

Jill and Wakon are also excellent parents and business owners/managers. Running a business involves a lot of responsibility. To be good at parenting and business management and blending the two is a real talent. It has been over three years since Evelyn and I have turned the business to our kids. It has run smoothly, professionally, and honorably. Wakon is an extremely hard and smart worker and the company has done very well. At times Wakon and I bump heads. We are both type A personalities, and this will happen at times. Jill and Wakon I am proud of you two.

Aiyana

Aiyana is their firstborn. Aiyana will turn seventeen this year and will be a senior in high school. Aiyana is sweet to everyone except Aidan. Aidan is Aiyana's thirteen-year-old brother. Both are at awkward ages, teenagers. Aiyana has a slight anxiety situation, nothing like her grandpa, and Aydan has a lot of nervous energy. If they are around each other at the wrong time they have a tendency not to be overly fond of one another. Overall, they are great kids. Aiyana was very outgoing as a youngster. She loved me to read to her and I would often tell her jokes. She would look up jokes and surprise me with one of them. She wasn't very interested in sports. She was a goalie in soccer and while attending the goal she would dance between the goalposts. She was bored. It turned out fine because she became my favorite dancer. She danced for MAPA, Maui Academy, and Performing Arts and they performed in many venues. She most often performed on the center stage of the Maui Mall. When we watched the dancers perform, I would get bored. The seats were uncomfortable, and the lighting wasn't very good but when Aiyana danced, I was comfortable, and I could see great. She made me proud. Her make-up, done by Jill, and her outfits, were so cute. At the end of her performance, she would greet our family and friends and in turn, we would adorn her with a kiss or a lei, and sometimes both. When Aiyana was in the 6th grade she got accepted at

Seabury Hall where her cousin Taysia was also attending. They would ride together and become real pals. Their school was a thirty-five-minute drive from Wailuku. Aiyana does well in school, and dance is her favorite extracurricular activity. She also likes theater since she was active in Maui Academy of Performing Arts (MAPA). Aiyana is a cute small girl, maybe ½ inch taller than her mom. She studies hard, gets good grades, and wants to attend college on the East Coast and become a design architect. I hope she chooses the West Coast for college,

Aidan

What a handful. When he came into this world he cried and hardly stopped for the first year and a half. He had volume. I felt sorry for Jill and anyone close to her. She and Wakon handled it well. Then Aidan saw the light. At about that age, Aidan started turning on every light switch that he could reach or climb to. He would flick it on and off as if discovered something, and he did. Then it became the ceiling fans, then the oven, then garbage trucks, and so on and so on. He is very bright and very curious and was very bratty. As he got older, he found more things to play with. It was the computer and iPhone that hooked him. Now he was out of sight and therefore out of mind. Sometimes I would see him on his desk near the front door. I would be in their kitchen and call out "Aidan." A little louder I would call, "Aidan." No response, so I would walk over to him, touch him and say "Aidan." He couldn't hear when he was on his computer. He can blank out everything, even Papa when he is playing his video games. It takes him ten minutes to do his homework and he also is going to Seabury Hall, a top curriculum college prep school. He is extremely bright but is not blue-collared and gets bored very easily. I think he could handle college physics at his current age if he applied himself. He is very handsome, with his beautiful blue eyes, and he is not a bad athlete. He does find time to play basketball, ping-pong and soccer; and we found out he is musically inclined and following his uncle Jeff in playing the piano. He has become very considerate and loving. I think he will excel at what he wants to do. MIT be prepared.

Alexa

Alexa, better known as Lexi, is the youngest of the Childers family. We had just consolidated the family business among Jill, Jeff, and Jennifer. Jill had given notice to her dentist that she was going to work in our family business. She came into the office and had a concerned look on her face. She looked at Evelyn and me and said, apologetically, "I'm pregnant." We were happy, but Jill felt it wasn't good timing. We cheered her up as it all turned out great. Lexi came into the world laughing and she made everyone else laugh and has continued to do so to this day. Lexi is funny and also very bright. Her best friend is her cousin Sisi, Jeff's youngest daughter. They go to Hongwanji together and are hard to separate when the day is over. Lexi is a real character and is almost always in a happy mood. I have only heard her cry once. Her attitude was completely opposite of Aidan's when he was her age.

Jeff and Amanda's and Children

We were visiting Jeff in Seattle and we met Amanda on their first date. Amanda is very pretty and smart. She had worked as a lead nurse at Seattle Children's Hospital where Jeff worked. They had informal lunches together in the hospital cafeteria. Their early conversations were friendly in 2004. There was a going-away party for one of the nurses at Jeff's house, and that is where they got to know each other better. They dated for three years. For one of those three years, they lived in San Diego to be close to Kai, Jeff's son from a previous marriage. Kai's stepfather was stationed there with Kai's mom, Michelle. While in San Diego, Jeff proposed to Amanda in 2008. He had purchased a small home in Lake Stevens, just north of Seattle just before meeting Amanda. He rented it when they were in San Diego and then returned to their house in 2009. They were married in our backyard. They stayed in Lake Stevens until Kai turned seventeen. That was the age Jeff was when he left Maui to go to college in Oregon.

Amanda gave birth to Gabriella, a beautiful baby girl. Evelyn and I would visit almost yearly. Ella and Kai were getting bigger, and we would enjoy them. On one trip Amanda told us she wasn't feeling well. She was getting migraine headaches and feeling anxious, and she had missed quite a bit of work recently. I felt sorry for her looking back at the problems I had with my depression and not finding proper medication. Mental illnesses and undiagnosed illnesses are so frustrating, and they are so misunderstood.

In 2016 Jeff brought Amanda, Ella, and Sisi to their new home, Maui. Jeff was going to make this big move and in addition to a career change from nursing to exterminating. We prefer to be called pest managers. We weren't sure if this was going to be a good fit, but he was willing to try. Also included in the move, were Amanda's mother, Debbie, and grandmother Gigi.

Jeff is a very good husband and father. He is also a good provider.

He has studied certain investments and has done very well. Tesla stock is his favorite. For my retirement party, he is going to give me an electric self-driving Tesla truck, but I think he is going to wait until my funeral.

We are certainly happy that Jeff made his decision to return. He has been a big asset to the company and Wakon and Jill, and we enjoy him and his family so much. Good news.... Amanda's condition was finally correctly diagnosed recently. She had a thyroid problem. All of her symptoms were not imaginary as some doctors implied. She had a simple operation that made her a different person.

Kainoa

Kainoa, whom we call Kai, is the oldest son of Jeff and Jeff's first wife Michelle. Michelle and Jeff met while Jeff was attending Oregon State University. Michelle was working at Noodle Me where Jeff was working part-time. Michelle got pregnant with Kai before their marriage when she was twenty years old, and Jeff was nineteen. I was upset with Jeff for not using birth control measures. I strongly suggested that he marry Michelle. He eventually did. I was the old-fashioned father forcing my will upon my son. Their marriage lasted less than two years. Despite it, Kai turned out to become a wonderful person. Kai lives with his mother Michelle, his stepfather, and his two brothers and a sister, when not attending school. When Jeff was living in the Seattle area, he would take every opportunity he could to be with Kai. After graduating from Linfield College as a registered nurse, Jeff moved to the Seattle area while Kai and Michelle were living near Spokane, Washington. His drive was nearly 300 miles one way, and it took about four hours. Jeff and Kai are very close like best friends close. They would go to all the skateboard parks, play basketball, play music, or just hang out. Kai usually comes to Hawaii one or two times a year. When Jeff and Amanda got married, Kai would often stay at their home. When he was young, Kai had some anxiety. He continually washed his hands. His hands were always clean and mine were always dirty. He is musically gifted and a good athlete like his dad. In his senior year in high school, his football team took league champs. Jeff and I flew from Maui to watch him play. He was a middle linebacker like I was in high school. The difference was his playing weight was 180 pounds and mine 145 pounds and they were on a rigid weight training program. He also is much better looking. They won that game to become state champs in their division. He chose to attend Whitworth University, a small college near Spokane. He considered becoming a doctor, but Jeff talked him out of it. Jeff feels that the life of a doctor is too stressful. Instead of seeking an MD, Kai would like to be a high school teacher and a coach. He is in his senior year of college so will go on to get his master's in education. I am confident that he will obtain his goal. We got a copy of his last semester's grades. He got a 4.0 GPA. Good job Kai.

Gabriella and Sienna (Sisi)

Gabriella, better known as Ella, is blond with blue eyes, very energetic, and a high achiever. She is a lucky girl along with her sister Sienna, better known as Sisi because they get a lot of attention from Amanda and Jeff. Amanda is a stay-at-home mom and is always doing creative things with the two of them. Sisi is five years old and also blond and with blue eyes. You would never know they are one-fourth Filipino. Ella is more on the precocious side. She learns very quickly and has a lot of curiosity and loves to read. When Ella puts her mind to it, and she often does, she can achieve. She was fluently reading by the time she got into first grade, and she was advanced in gymnastics and Tahitian dance. She is in second grade. Sisi, on the other hand, takes her time doing things. She still waits until Amanda spoon feeds her. She is not lazy, and she is not slow but is an opportunist. Her attitude is "if I can get Mommy to do it for me, why not.?" Her best friend is Lexi, and they play so well together and go to school together at Puu Kakui Elementary. Playing together sometimes involves screaming, which apparently, they love, and I hate. My old ears are sensitive to their excitement, although, I know they both are on the right path to happiness and success.

Evelyn, my wonderful and caring wife:

By the time this book is in print, Evelyn and I will have been married forty-eight years. We both look forward to our 50th and possibly our 60th, and unlikely, but slightly possible, our 70th. Both our parents were married for close to sixty years until one of the spouses passed on. When we pass on, I have planned, with Evelyn's blessing, that we go together. The Waiehu Stream runs parallel to the back of our property. I plan that we have a "Celebration of Life" and our ashes will be combined and set afloat down the Waiehu Stream to the Pacific Ocean. How romantic and how beautiful. I am looking forward to being there with Evelyn.

A lot has happened in forty-seven-plus years. We have the most fantastic family ever. Our kids and grandkids are wonderful. Evelyn is a super caring wife, mom, and Grammy. Her life revolves around our family and me and our family revolves around her. Our family is our best friends. We truly love each other and trust each other. Living in Maui is so special, especially when your kids and grandkids live within minutes. Evelyn has made my life much more meaningful than before I married her. She supported me and encouraged me when I was depressed. She rooted me on when I ran, and she worked by my side for over thirty years, and sometimes she never got compensated. She is still working along with me. We enjoy working with the kids in the business, and our extended family, our employees. We could retire but choose not to. We will gradually reduce our work time. She worked with me on the yard for many years until that became our main source of arguing. She thought she was in charge of my yard. If she built all the rock walls, I may have had a different viewpoint. She drove me crazy sometimes. One time she pulled out many of my prize plants and that was it. No mas! Kaput! And some words I don't want in print. I told her that was it. I did not want her help in the yard anymore. We get along better regarding the yard; however, she is now very critical of everything I do in it.

My yard is my pride and joy. I spend close to fifteen hours per week working for perfection. She can ruin that in a single sentence. One time I finished a hard day in the yard, and I was very proud of what I did. Her comment as I came in was, "Why do you always move your mouth up and down when you're working in the yard? You look like an old man. "Her good outweighs her bad. She has dinner ready; the house is all clean, my medicine is prepared, and generally, all I have to do when I enter the house is eat and relax. Evelyn and I are both very lucky. Our kids and grandkids are such an inspiration. One of my hopes is that all the grandkids choose to get married in our backyard.

A project Evelyn took up when I started this book was to sew masks to protect from Covid. She sewed over 300 and would give them to the grandkids, our kids, and anyone she felt was deserving. We are both slowing down now. I am working three days a week and she is working four days a week but, she goes in on her day off. We walk five or six days a week, three miles at a clip. We have a new walking partner now, Eric Taketa. Eric became a close walking friend of Tom and me about three years ago. Our morning walks are rather rigorous. We start at Jenifer's house and end after we have ascended two high hills and re-ascend one. It is a good workout and we generally do it around sixteen to seventeen minutes per mile pace, with Eric around seventeen minutes per mile, not quite as fast as the 6:30 pace that I ran in the Honolulu Marathon in 1981. I am forty years older and slowing down a bit. During our walks, we get into some very interesting conversations.

I am at the most contented time in my life. At one time we owned four houses, two businesses and I was bipolar and had a seizure history and memory lapses. It didn't work well for me. I was too stressed. Now we own one small house on the Big Island. Our property and business have been given to our kids with their permission to allow us to live in it until we no longer can. We can quit work when we want to. I am on proper medication thanks to Evelyn. I have been seizure-free for 18 years and I have not been depressed or manic for about ten years. Now with more time, we can travel more, I can play in my yard more and write more.

With the warmest Aloha, Bruce, and Evelyn

Printed in the USA
CPSIA information can be obtained
at www.ICGtesting.com
LVHW021324110924
790643LV00014B/762

9 798886 041521